JUSTPEACE ETHICS

Cascade Companions

The Christian theological tradition provides an embarrassment of riches: from scripture to modern scholarship, we are blessed with a vast and complex theological inheritance. And yet this feast of traditional riches is too frequently inaccessible to the general reader.

The Cascade Companions series addresses the challenge by publishing books that combine academic rigor with broad appeal and readability. They aim to introduce nonspecialist readers to that vital storehouse of authors, documents, themes, histories, arguments, and movements that comprise this heritage with brief yet compelling volumes.

TITLES IN THIS SERIES:

FORTHCOMING TITLES:

Justpeace Ethics

A Guide to Restorative Justice and Peacebuilding

JAREM SAWATSKY

With a Foreword by HOWARD ZEHR

 CASCADE *Books* · Eugene, Oregon

JUSTPEACE ETHICS
A Guide to Restorative Justice and Peacebuilding

Cascade Companions 7

Cascade Books
A Division of Wipf and Stock Publishers
199 W. 8th Ave., Suite 3
Eugene, OR 97401

www.wipfandstock.com

ISBN 13: 978-1-55635-299-7

Cataloging-in-Publication data:

Sawatsky, Jarem.

Justpeace ethics : a guide to restorative justice and peacebuilding / Jarem
Sawatsky.

xvi + 98 p. ; cm. —Includes bibliographical references.

Cascade Companions 7

ISBN 13: 978-1-55635-299-7

1. Restorative justice. 2. Peace. 3. Conflict Management I. Zehr, Howard.
II. Title. III. Series.

HV8688 .S28 2008

Manufactured in the U.S.A.

Contents

Foreword

Over the past few decades, a number of overlapping fields of study and practice have emerged in the quest for just and peaceful societies. This is illustrated by developments at the Center for Justice & Peacebuilding (CJP) where I teach, and where Jarem received his master's degree.

Initially the CJP began as a "conflict-transformation" program aimed at widening and deepening the concept of conflict resolution. Then it expanded to include restorative justice, which is in many respects a peacebuilding approach to justice issues. But our graduate students, who are practitioners from all over the globe, come to us facing issues of trauma (often traumatized themselves), development, and a variety of organizational dynamics. So our program expanded to include these fields as well. We began to recognize that these fields of study fit together into a whole; each had something important to contribute and was, in fact, a subfield under a larger peacebuilding umbrella.[1] Our founding director, John Paul Lederach, termed this overall vision "justpeace."

Each of these approaches or subfields addresses some critical part required to build a peaceful world. But each of these fields has its own history and perspectives, and often

1. See, for example, Schirch, *Little Book of Strategic Peacebuilding*.

these are not integrated. In 2007, one of our graduate students, Matthew Hartman, decided that it was high time the various components of this overall peacebuilding field talk to each other. A "palaver" or dialogue that he organized brought faculty who worked in these fields together for several days to explore our points of connection and dissonance. One of our discoveries was that conflict transformation and related fields were strong on theories but had very little explicit focus on values. Restorative justice, on the other hand, was big on values. Moreover, even restorative justice needed to explore its values more explicitly.

To be honest, my own recognition of the importance of values was somewhat belated. In the early 1980s when some of us were formulating the basic concept and principles of restorative justice, we were primarily trying to communicate what we were doing in practice. The conceptual framework, then, grew out of practice and was intended more to communicate than theorize. We assumed values were important, but we didn't talk much about them. Increasingly, however, I have become convinced that naming, exploring, and being guided by explicit values is absolutely essential.

I have long been concerned about the tendency of all interventions, no matter how well intended, to go astray. As I frequently tell my classes, all interventions, no matter how well intended, have unintended consequences. Faced with these tendencies, then, it is important that our practice be guided by explicit principles. But increasingly I have become aware—and again based on observed practice—that even principles are not enough; we can espouse wonderful principles and yet do some terrible things if our principles and our practices are not consciously grounded in values.

This is true not only for restorative justice but for all of peacebuilding. That is why Jarem's work is so important. Interestingly, as he says in his introduction, this work began by listening to these various components of peacebuilding that are brought together in our program. What he found was that we did share a common set of values that were, however, more implicit than explicit. But he went beyond naming those values, putting them into a holistic framework of paired values in which one value counters the possible excesses or abuses of another. The value of interconnectedness is important, for instance, but by itself can lead to excessive stress on the community and universality. By pairing it with "particularity" (a profound acknowledgement of the importance of the individual and the context), a balance is found. It is a dynamic relationship that acknowledges the importance of both individual identity and solidarity with one another. This is a more sophisticated and nuanced approach to values than is normally taken.

Coincidentally, perhaps, on the day that I reviewed this manuscript I also read two other manuscripts from our graduates, both exploring some aspect of the values that underlie restorative justice. Both suggested, as Jarem does, that restorative justice and peacebuilding in general are much more than a way to intervene in situations of wrongdoing or conflict; rather, justpeace is a way of life. What this suggests is that the values and principles of justpeace can provide us a vision of how we want to live together as well as specific suggestions about how we do so.

At any rate, as the field of justpeacebuilding continues to grow, a discussion of values is essential. This book makes a huge contribution to this dialogue.

Howard Zehr
Professor of Restorative Justice
Center for Justice & Peacebuilding
Eastern Mennonite University
Harrisonburg, Virginia

Preface

This short book started around the year 2000 as an interview project. I was a graduate student at the conflict-transformation program at Eastern Mennonite University where the two streams of peace studies and justice studies were held together in one program. In the one stream, scholar-practitioners were engaged in international peacebuilding and in the work of conflict transformation. In the other scholar-practitioners were working at restorative justice. These two groups worked in different contexts, with different methods and with somewhat different goals. Yet they knew that at some level they had much in common. The goal of my research project was to test if there was some kind of shared imagination that guided their work. I interviewed faculty and surveyed much literature and tried to come up with a way of speaking about the shared imagination that guided their work. The goal was to listen to people who were acting their way into a new way of thinking. The goal was to learn how thought and action overlapped, or how those working at the concrete practice of peace and justice engaged and incarnated peace and justice in settings of conflict and violence. What emerged we called the justpeace ethic.[1]

1. Sawatsky, "JustPeace Ethic."

As I began to deepen my understanding and practice of peace and restorative justice, I often came back to those guiding virtues—to analyze a conflict, to design a peacebuilding project, to evaluate restorative-justice literature, to teach the heart of peacebuilding and restorative justice to undergraduate students. I realized the justpeace ethic that had emerged through the interview project had connections and ramifications well beyond the narrow context from which it first arose. The second manifestation of the project was to expand the project from a narrow interview project of like-minded people, namely Christian (Mennonite) peace and justice workers, to a more general audience and focus, namely, the restorative justice movement. With the help of a grant from Menno Simons College, I attended the sixth International Conference on Restorative Justice, where I presented the paper "Restorative Values: Where Means and Ends Converge."[2] This was an attempt to show how the practices and theories of restorative justice could be both understood and challenged from the perspective of the guiding virtues. That paper was well received. Simon Fraser University put the paper on their most-popular-essays Web site.[3]

I started hearing from a diverse collection of people on how helpful the paper was to them: the Thames Valley Police in the United Kingdom, a traditional elder from a First Nations group in Canada, a Chilean domestic-abuse recovery program, a high school alternative-justice measures program. And Howard Zehr kept urging me to find some way to share this framework more broadly. I knew I needed to take the project a step further.

2. Sawatsky, "Restorative Values."
3. Online: http://www.sfu.ca/cfrj/popular.html.

This third manifestation is in your hands. In this short book I try to bring together the past versions with a fresh approach and focus. This book is written as a guide to moral thinking and acting as it relates to peace- and justice build-ing. The taking-off point is still the virtues that guide the work of justice building and peacebuilding, but by now my understanding of these virtues has been further shaped by the people I have shared my life with. These include people of many different faith or spiritual traditions. I am a Christian peacebuilder deeply influenced by my Mennonite roots. This particular orientation has led me to be keen to learn how God has moved in and through other faith traditions. My work and research have allowed me to explore some of these connec-tions in relation to a range of other faith traditions. These ex-plorations inform and sometimes even transform how I read, participate, and practice within the Christian tradition. This book then is also a result of such spiritual cross-fertilization.

In this short book I try to highlight how a justpeace ethic comes out of grassroots practitioners, connects with a broad section of scholars and practitioners, and draws on various faith traditions. My hope is that it creates a fruitful meeting space where people from diverse traditions can hold on to their particularity while drawing on common aspects of a shared imagination of just peacebuilding. Such a space might open up paths for more fruitful peacebuilding.

Included in this book are ten sections of questions re-lated to ten virtues of justpeace building. For each section, I list a number of questions arising out of the virtue. These questions are an attempt to let the light of this virtue shine on various aspects of our imagination and work. Each section asks questions about eliciting vision, about design issues of peace and justice initiatives, about intervention issues, and about evaluation issues. Practitioners or scholars of peace and restorative justice can use these questions as they try to embody justpeace within a particular location. Church groups and other communities can also use these questions as they reflect on the resources within their communities that might lead to justpeace.

As a Mennonite Christian, I try to draw out some of the aspects of my traditions that come into focus as one looks through the lens of justpeace ethics. I try to point toward ways that other faith traditions also share some of these teachings, but it is, of course, up to people from those traditions to decide if the justpeace ethic presented here is indeed shared territory that could act as a meeting place for people from diverse backgrounds.

I must thank my friends, colleagues, and teachers at Eastern Mennonite University's Center for Justice and Peacebuilding, who were the first to be interviewed for this project, especially Hizkias Assefa, Ron Kraybill, John Paul Lederach, Akum Longchari, Lisa Schirch, Nancy Sider, and Howard Zehr.

I also need to thank my colleagues and students at Canadian Mennonite University who have given me the time, space, and feedback necessary to bring this work to this point.

This book was written and researched over many years and in at least four countries. There are too many people to thank who offered assistance—whether insight from their practice, a pleasant place to write, or wonderful conversation and coffee. I warmly acknowledge those unnamed friends.

I want to acknowledge Albert Labun, who has carefully and insightfully edited a number of versions of this book. I also thank all the people at Cascade Books, who worked hard behind the scenes to bring you this book.

Finally to my church community, Grain of Wheat, and my family, especially Rhona and my two girls, I want to thank you for accompanying me and shaping me on this journey toward justpeace.

ONE

An Overview of a Justpeace Ethic

THE NEED TO ARTICULATE JUSTPEACE VIRTUES

A group of justice, law, and conflict practitioners gather for a training workshop. We go around the circle introducing ourselves and sharing a story of a firsthand experience of either justice or injustice. When the circle ends, we've heard twenty stories of injustice and no stories of justice. What's going on here? Why do people working in justice and peacebuilding have no stories of times they have touched and tasted justice?

I've repeated this exercise at the start of numerous workshops and trainings with a great variety of people. The results are always similar. It seems that we have a far keener sense of injustice than of justice. The stories of injustice are painful stories of being excluded, of being shamed, of being broken, of being violated, of losing yourself. So why are these stories more readily shared than stories of justice? I suspect that we don't know what justice is, and deep down we might believe that justice is as ugly as injustice. Watch TV for one evening, and each time the word "justice" is used, listen for the implications. Usually when we "bring someone to justice," we mean throwing them in jail, exacting revenge. Sometimes it even means to kill the person. No wonder we steer clear of experiences of justice. In the experience of victims, offenders, and communities, ugly justice reflects the same painful characteristics as injustice: exclusion, shame, violation, broken identity. Ivan Illich, theologian and philosopher, says that this is a defining characteristic of modern institutions; they accomplish the opposite of their stated goals.[1] Education makes you dumb, hospitals make you sick, national security makes the nation less secure, traffic control creates congestion, and the justice system creates injustice.

But what if justice isn't ugly? What if justice is something beautiful and whole? If injustice is about excluding, taking way, breaking, and being shamed, then shouldn't justice be more about embracing, giving back, connecting, and becoming radiant? If injustice is about losing identity, shouldn't justice be about rediscovering identity?

The term "justpeace" reminds us that justice and peace belong together and are essentially inseparable. Peace without justice is suppression. Justice without peace is a new form of oppression. Justice and peace belong together. The term "justpeace" has been borrowed from other thinkers.[2] It is used to point toward a different kind of justice and peace, one where, as in Psalm 85, "truth and mercy have met together, justice and peace have kissed."[3]

We have so many misconceptions of the essential nature of justice and peace that we need guidance in how to work at

1. Illich, *Deschooling Society*.

2. See Moltmann, *Creating a Just Future*; see also Lederach, "Justpeace."

3. Lederach, "Truth and Mercy."

justice building and peacebuilding. Many longstanding traditions within states, churches, and other faith groups have in fact taught us that justice is essentially about the same qualities as injustice. We have often nurtured bitterness and discontent. We need wise guides to help us engage and embody ways that cultivate the fruit of justice, what Martin Luther King Jr. argued was "the creation of the beloved community."[4]

Often justice and peace have been used as tools of statecraft to keep the state system functioning. This is indeed a kind of peace, but it is a state of being that can be settled in a peace settlement or peace accord, with the hope that some day peace will trickle down to the grassroots. Furthermore, this kind of justice is about handling disputes in such a way as to build the strength of the state, sometimes at the expense of communities, victims, and offenders.[5] The justpeace ethic presented here plots a different path, one not so much informed by blind-lady justice, the state mascot and symbol of justice. We will explore this symbol later, but let the reader be warned that this guide draws on a different imagination. The biblical prophet Amos described justice as rolling down a mountain like a river, and righteousness as an ever-flowing stream (5:24). Here justice is dynamic rather than static. This justice is made by God rather than by humans, and it is based in relationship rather than impartiality. It cultivates beauty and change rather than balancing the scales of pain. From this perspective, the goal of restorative justice and peacebuilding is not merely to fine-tune the current systems by adding new models and techniques to control behavior. The current

4. King, "Nonviolence and Racial Justice," 8.

5. Christie, "Conflict as Property"; Pranis, et al., *Peacemaking Circles*.

systems are not based on values that can end the pain they have helped to create. Restorative justice and peacebuilding, at least as practiced by these engaged Christians, is rooted in a wholly different imagination and worldview. It offers an alternative to the basic assumptions underlying the modern state system. It offers a different set of virtues and assumptions for imagining and engaging the world.

A third reason why we need good guides is that Christian theology and practice have advocated many essentially violent understandings of peace and justice that have created devastation around the world. Whether this devastation is from the linking of Christianity to colonialism or from disconnecting notions of righteousness and mercy from justice and peace, through the centuries Christians have justified mass violence in the name of building peace and justice in the world. This guide draws on Christians who are deeply pained by their own tradition and yet rely on their faith understandings in ways that go home in shalom. This vision of working through conflicts in ways that all go home in shalom—in right relationship with land, God, self, neighbor, stranger, and even enemy—is one of biblical visions of responding to harms in community (Exod 18:23). This vision shapes this guide.

Where do we start? The international expansion of the restorative-justice movement is a hopeful sign of a readiness and a yearning for a different orientation to justice. I attribute the incredible growth of restorative justice across nations, cultures, faith traditions and sociopolitical contexts to the belief that restorative justice connects with something: with something old, something common, and something intuitively right, within people from widely diverse backgrounds. I believe this connecting point is a common set of ancient virtues we still carry with us. These are virtues not just about how to approach conflict but about how to live life in its fullest.

Yet we so often lose sight of these virtues. I've watched compassionate people enter into conflict and apply the tools and techniques of conflict intervention, and in the process totally lose sight of the people involved. Too often our conflict design, intervention, and evaluation lead us away from the actual experience of the people most affected by conflict. When this happens, peace accords fail to cultivate peace at the grassroots, and offenders and communities become re-offended by our response to harms.

Although many people speak of restorative justice and peacebuilding as a values-based or a principles-based movement, few have offered a coherent articulation of those values. Without such a clear articulation, these fields are susceptible to cooptation and to technique proliferation. Without understanding how restorative-justice processes are rooted in particular virtues, one is tempted to use them in inappropriate ways. When the field expands without such an understanding, we tend to collect techniques and processes without having the imagination to know how to most fruitfully relate to them.

Too often when we institutionalize these virtues, they become tools of oppression and control rather than empowerment. When we universalize methods, we unhook them from their context, their virtues, their narrative roots, and the means that give them birth. By universalizing methods, we impose them on new situations that they may not fit. In this book I attempt to articulate these virtues in such a way as to open up space for listening, discovering, and rediscovering ways of becoming peace and justice in the midst of conflict. I attempt to create a fruitful meeting ground for people of very diverse backgrounds. By being clear about the virtues underlying peacebuilding and restorative justice, we can create practical ways to root peacebuilding in the very character of the peace and justice we hope to achieve. My agenda is to call people into a creative and wise search for a beautiful justice and a respect for all of humanity and all creation.

A VIRTUES-BASED APPROACH

This justpeace ethic tries to root peacebuilding, conflict transformation, and restorative justice in the very character of the kind of peace and justice that we are working towards. Put differently, those who use such an ethic or imagination begin with some particular vision of the good life or of the fullness of life. This ethics guides creates space to explore questions about the meaning of that good, full life. It comes from particular understandings of the nature of life and the deepest truth of our identity. This is the starting point of the model and is explored more fully in chapter 2. This vision does not function as some distant shore, but is something that we strive to reach with each step. The means of getting to justpeace is the same as justpeace. We will return to this idea.

In contrast, much criminal justice assumes that we can achieve justice and the common good through dishing out pain and punishment to rule breakers. Much foreign policy also reflects this same logic: that state violence is sometimes needed to return others to the path to peace and justice. In these settings, virtues of love, kindness, and compassion are sometimes applied to the immediate family but not to the enemy, the stranger, the alien, or the neighbor. The "family-values" movement is a good example of this orientation. We love those who love us in return but assume that love can't shape our economic, political, or ecological practices. We hand over to secular experts those people who fall into the theological categories of the enemy, the stranger, the alien, the neighbor, and even the self. Sometimes when we stop treating them through a theological understanding, we also stop treating them with the compassion we expect within a faith orientation.

The justpeace ethic is an ethical guide of a different sort. The focus in this ethical model is not on following preset rules about what is or is not allowed, as is the case within criminal justice. Neither is the focus primarily on fulfilling some kind of a duty or idea of what is valued at the moment. Rather the focus is on creating people with an imagination and a character that has the capacity to respond wisely to the diversity and complexity of life.

Within philosophical discourse, this kind of ethics is often considered virtue ethics. It begins with a particular understanding of the good life and builds toward practices, habits, and behaviors that embody the character and characteristics of the good life. In Western discourse virtue ethics goes back to Plato and Aristotle. It was introduced into Christian circles by Augustine but soon became unfashionable. Only recently have philosophers and theologians returned to this approach.[6]

The virtue-based ethical approach has also been used outside Western and Christian traditions. Confucianism used it in China. Examples of it occur among Canadian Aboriginal peoples.[7] For example, the Anishinabie had

6. See the work of Alasdair MacIntyre (*After Virtue*), John Howard Yoder (*Politics of Jesus*), and Stanley Hauerwas (*Community of Character*).

7. I have used the word *Aboriginal* as a respectful way to speak of the indigenous peoples of North America. In the United States the term

a central idea of the good life, called *p'mad'ziwin*, out of which they derived the seven sacred laws (love, respect, courage, honesty, wisdom, humility, and truth).[8] In the Engaged Buddhist context, nirvana serves as something that can be touched with each step in this world. An ethical way of being in the world is arrived at through seeking to embody the end the true nature of life with each step.[9] One of the central challenges of virtue ethics is to determine who decides which virtues, and whose common good we are working towards. Each virtue-ethical system has a different set of virtues. Moreover, in some settings the virtues are designed to create good citizens (Aristotelianism or Confucianism) whereas in other systems, following the virtues might mean being killed (martyred) by the state.[10] Alasdair MacIntyre argues that virtue ethics must emerge from communities that practice them.[11] Therefore my own research did not begin with a preset list of possible virtues to be tested in the field. Rather the beginning was at the grassroots, listening to respected, engaged Christian peacebuilders and restorative-justice practitioners. Then the community of

---

used is *American Indian*. In Canada, the normal usage is *Aboriginal*. What constitutes respectful and appropriate language is in flux. Here I have deviated from the *Oxford English Dictionary* and public media usage, which would lowercase the word *aboriginal*. In this book, however, *Aboriginal* denotes the name of a people, a nation. In a similar way, the word *Canadian* is capitalized.

8. Sivell-Ferri, "Ojibwa Circle"; Couture, *Cost-Benefit Analysis*; Sawatsky, *Ethic of Traditional Communities*.

9. Dalai Lama XIV, *Ethics for the New Millennium*; and Hanh, *For a Future*.

10. See the work of John Howard Yoder (*Politics of Jesus*), Hauerwas (*Community of Character*), and Hanh (*Fragrant Palm Leaves*).

11. MacIntyre, *After Virtue*.

listening was widened to include others working at the intersection or the overlapping of justice and peace (justpeace). The virtues that emerge are not the same as the ones of a philosopher king (Plato). Where there is overlap with other lists of virtues, this one emerges from a careful listening to those who practice justpeace. Some are recognizable as common virtues and some are harder to recognize. But each virtue guides practitioners of justpeace as they create interesting experiments with truth.

Before we explore the virtues that emerge from such a process, it is important to highlight more fully where and how these virtues are located.

Our actions spring out of our virtues and our vices. Actions don't come out of nowhere. They take shape because of how we understand the world. Our virtues are part of the lens that shapes our understanding of the world. However, virtues have roots. Our virtues are rooted in and inspired by particular stories, cultures, and narratives. We might understand the relationship like this:

Observables—context, language, technique, action

Ethics—virtues—guiding principles

Narrative—religion, culture, community, that which inspires and motivates at the deepest level

Realm of commonality

Figure 1—Construction of Meaning

The small triangle at the top of the diamond is that which is visible. We see the actions. In justice and peace contexts, we see processes and techniques, and we hear particular language. However, this is only the tip of the iceberg. Actions come from virtues, and virtues in turn come from narrative. This is important to understand, as there are many who would argue that we can simply import and export processes and virtues across contexts. This diagram illustrates why such an approach is problematic.

When virtues become unhooked from these narrative contexts, all sorts of trouble unfolds: foreign virtues and techniques are imposed on peoples, local stories and traditions are co-opted and used for control or are forgotten, voices from particular traditions are silenced in the name of nondiscrimination.

When the Royal Canadian Mounted Police brought Family Group Conferencing (Australian style) to Canada, they claimed the technique was a good fit for Aboriginal people, as it was based on traditional Maori virtues. However, some Canadian Aboriginal people saw it as a top-down "appropriation of culture which exploits indigenous knowledge and spirituality in order to meet government bureaucratic policy and goals."[12] This is precisely the kind of damage that happens when virtues are unhooked from contexts, universalized, and then imposed.

The concept of justpeace virtues is very important as a shared meeting ground for people from diverse backgrounds. The goal here is not to get agreement on universal liberal values. The goal is to create space where people from diverse identity groups and working in diverse contexts are

12. Lee, "Newest Old Gem," 310.

able to draw deeply from their particularity while at the same time addressing their common connections. In Figure 1 ("Construction of Meaning"), the width of the diamond is the realm of commonness. As one dives deeply into the narrative, there is little room for shared experience. Either you share those stories, or you don't. For example, my narrative context is shaped by the Christian tradition and, within that, by the Mennonite tradition. These stories inform what virtues I can recognize as part of the path of justpeace. Although many do not share this particular narrative context, they may well share very similar virtues. Likewise in Figure 1, if you move up to the top of what is observable about the context, there is little room to share. Either you use that language and those techniques in those contexts, or you don't. For example, observing a Family Group Conference on a Maori *marae* is a very different experience from observing a Rwandan *gacaca*. The techniques, processes, and contexts are very different. Yet under the surface we may identity common justpeace virtues and a common justpeace imagination. The widest part of the diamond, the place where there is the most room for people to stand together, is at the level of virtues.

I believe we are deeply spiritual, story-formed peoples. For justice and peace to bloom, we must draw deeply from the roots of our own traditions, and we must also connect with peoples unlike us. Focusing on virtues can create space for fruitful dialogue and creative, collaborative action; but such a virtues approach has life only as people draw from their traditions. Focusing on virtues is an attempt to take traditional teachings as the basis for peace-and-justice activities and must not be used to co-opt or silence traditional teachings.

Figure 2 demonstrates this relationship.

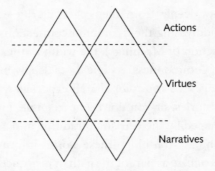

Actions

Virtues

Narratives

Figure 2—Different narratives, different points of application, sharing a common ethic

The two diamonds can represent two different religious traditions that are active in different contexts and open the possibility that they share a common ethic. Figure 2 does not intend to suggest that people from different narrative contexts actually share a common ethic but, rather, to demonstrate that they could have basic similarities even as they differ significantly in outward form and in the stories that guide them.

If it is true that common virtues are a potential meeting place for different traditions, then ethics (the dialogue of what guides action) could provide a powerful meeting place for different disciplines or even different religious traditions that are interested in peace and justice work. Justpeace ethics attempts to create such a space.

THE JOURNEY WHERE ENDS AND MEANS ARE THE SAME . . .

We must return now to the idea that ends and means should be the same. When *how* we do something (the means) is disconnected from *what* we hope to accomplish (the end), we can justify all sorts of harmful behavior that is abhorrent even to ourselves. We mistakenly expect that low-bar methods will achieve high-bar ends. Killing is okay if it is for peace. Harming victims is not okay, but harming offenders is okay because it teaches a lesson. If we apply this punishment now, we will get peace later. If we bomb them now, they won't bomb us later. It is okay to mine the earth's resources unsustainably (means) if I get some advantage (end).

We do this in many less-dramatic ways. We desire healthy relationships between people (end) and think the way to get them is to deal rationally with the issues (means). Although dealing rationally with issues can be a good thing, it can also alienate us from our whole selves. Thereby we exclude those elements that are not rational and those dynamics that are not issue-oriented.

Many of the great peacebuilders have been inspired by a radically different perspective. Gandhi said it this way: "Become the change you desire."[13] The renowned Buddhist peacebuilder Thich Nhat Hanh says that there is no way to peace, but that peace is the way. Jesus said it in his challenge

13. On the Web site http://www.quoteland.com, the editor of *The Yale Book of Quotations*, Fred R. Shapiro, wrote on July 26, 2007: "The recently published *Yale Book of Quotations* has the following: 'We must be the change we wish to see in the world.' Quoted in L.A. *Times*, 30 July 1989. According to the Gandhi Institute for Nonviolence, this has not been traced in Gandhi's writings but 'the Gandhi family states that M. K. Gandhi was known to say this verse many times in his lifetime and believes it to be original with him'" (http://forum.quoteland.com/1/OpenTopic?a=tpc&s=586192041&f=099191541&m=1541945383).

to "love your enemies" and in his call to incarnate "the way, the truth and the life" in the present moment of one's existence. Uniting ends and means is both a social critique and an inspiring way to live. When people and the earth are seen as means, then they are discardable, like a resource to use up on the way to getting somewhere else. When seen as ends, they must be held in great respect.

The only way to get to justpeace is to become justpeace. It is this imagination that leads the Dalai Lama to say that global transformation comes through inner transformation. Peace is not a distant goal, but something we must live and breathe in the way we live our lives. There is no unjust path that leads to justice.

What does this mean for restorative justice and peace-building? Restorative justice cannot be confined to petty, first-time young offenders. Similarly, peacebuilding is not just a postconflict activity. Restorative justice and peacebuilding are not narrow methods for how to respond to certain types of conflicts. Rather they represent a view of life and a way of life. The same virtues that guide our conflict work should also guide our organizational structures and our purchasing habits. In this way, integrated virtues for life guide both our means and our ends.

We see this powerfully where victim, offender, and community gather together to learn to see each other and to meaningfully address harm. Here the process of encounter has the same characteristics as the end goal: compassion, truth, responsibility, accountability. This ends/means consistency is strikingly absent in a courtroom, where lawyers argue in front of judges, and where victims, offenders, and communities often remain silent. Being silent observers is not the end we desire for victims, offenders, or communities. An ends/means consistency is also absent whenever we use violence to try to achieve peace.

The journey of raising the bar of means to become the ends must be one of humble evaluation. Gandhi saw that if he sought truth, then his methods must also be truthful. To walk this path with integrity is to admit that we are a mix of truth and untruth. We need to work together with a discerning community and with those with whom we are in conflict in order to determine a truthful path. This is why Gandhi saw this life as an experiment in truth. Part of what we think is truth now is untruth. To unite ends and means is to become what you desire while at the same time recognizing that you are not what you think you are. This is true for victim, community, offender, and peacebuilding facilitator. The goal of our focus on justpeace virtues, then, is to guide us as we become experiments with truth.

WHEN JUSTICE IS CREATED, NOT SERVED . . .

When justice is served, it is something that you are brought to, often unwillingly, and that is then imposed on you. When justice is served, it is often an ugly justice. However, when justice is created through engaging experiments with truth, something new, something beautiful is given space to emerge out of the brokenness of harm. The imagination of justice and peace as something that is served stands in contrast with a justpeace that is co-created.

When justice is served . . .	When justice is cocreated . . .
Participants are passive-aggressive adversaries.	Participants are active, collaborative "healers" and work together to address harms and to rebuild relationships.
Justice gets handed out in a one-size-fits-all manner by neutral, impartial, third-party experts.	Justice gets created and drawn out by those most involved in the harm, sometimes helped along by a trusted facilitator.
Justice is a rules-based response focusing on facts and punishment.	Justice is a caring response that holds people in respect while supporting them to (re)discover who they are.
Justice is a narrow approach focusing on dishing out punishment to offenders.	Justice is an expansive response that addresses both the specific harms and the root causes that may ripple through generations and whole structures
The goal is to suppress conflicts and to defend the current system, the status quo,	The goal is to enter into suffering and conflict and to explore together what needs to change to allow life to flow freely.
Justice is about appearing strong and knowing facts beyond the shadow of a doubt.	Justice is about becoming vulnerable and entering into self-doubt.
Justice is about powerful people controlling other people.	Justice is about listening and participating together to meet real needs.
Justice is about hating and harming the enemy.	Justice is moving toward love in our relationships and in our organizing.
Participants are silent and excluded by rigid processes	Participants' voices are included, and processes remain flexible to allow meaningful embrace of participants' identity and needs
The guilt and punishment of justice is something to be avoided, and a culture of nonresponsibility is perpetuated	Restitution and reintegration of victims and offenders create a new horizon when a culture of taking responsibility is encouraged.

When justice is created, it becomes a creative, almost sacred act of dancing our way back to humanity. It is about finding ourselves again. It is about learning to see the good and the bad in others and in ourselves. It is about strengthening community and learning to live with respect. This book is about drawing out and nurturing visions and quests for this deep, beautiful justpeace.

A Web of Virtues

If this beautiful justice truly challenges the dominant ways of understanding justice, then it is important that we find ways of talking about justpeace virtues without doing violence to the concept of justpeace. If we believe that peace and justice are more about putting things together than breaking them apart, more about relationships than abstractions, more about wholeness than fragmentation, then how do we talk about core virtues? To conceptualize life as virtues is already to play the modern game—to rationalize, break apart, and abstract. How do we speak of the new, or even the ancient, way without falling into the modern trap?

Rather than speaking of virtues in a hierarchical fashion or in isolation, we will examine how justpeace virtues are linked together in a web of interrelated virtues. Three concentric circles illustrate the ripples of interconnected virtues. The circle has long been held as a symbol of life, of healing, and of wholeness. Pairs of justpeace virtues are held together in creative tension to help remind us of the complexity of life but also to equip us in our experiments with truth. One of Aristotle's virtues was the mean, or the narrow space, between two vices or corresponding excesses. On the one hand, this tightrope approach to ethics often leaves us fearful and sometimes paralyzed. On the other hand, when we hold two virtues in tension, a new horizon or field of play emerges. This is more like a meadow that we are invited to explore and to play in, where we can cultivate wise experiments with truth. Figure 3 illustrates these relationships.

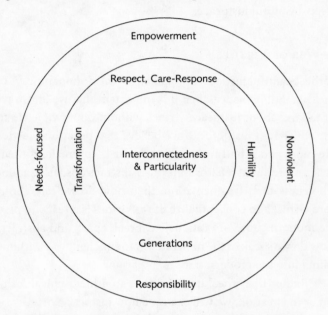

Figure 3—A Justpeace Ethic: Linking Guiding Virtues

Chapter 2 carries the title "The Heart of the Matter: Interconnectedness and Particularity." The virtue called inter-connectedness is a holistic view that all things are connected to each other in a web of relationships. Justpeace comes down to right relationships between all (people, land, structures, God). A harm or crime creates ripples of disruption to many relationships. Interconnectedness confronts injustice (harms) with the goal of establishing a just connection.

The virtue called particularity respects particular identity. Particularity recognizes that context, culture, and time are all relevant matters of justice. Particularity says that we are not all the same. It is about respecting diversity and difference. Justpeace does not have a single source but comes from many communities.

Interconnectedness says that we are connected, and that harms create responsibility to those affected (victims, community, family). Particularity adds that while we are connected, we are not all the same. Justice must respect both our connections and our particularity.

Chapter 3 highlights the virtues that lead to a people-focused approach to change. The first linked virtue pair is personal care-response and generations lens.

The virtue called personal care-response calls for justpeace to be oriented around human qualities of care rather than rules-responses or rights-responses. It sees each person as inherently worthy of respect. To harms, it searches for responses that care for real people and relationships, especially for the victims, offenders, and communities. This virtue sees crime as not against the state but against people.

Having the perspective of a generations lens is a relational virtue with a long-term time dimension. A generations lens looks both to the past and to the future to determine the best way to relate to the present. This virtue is interested in causes of harms, both personal and structural. It is also interested in how our responses to harms today affect the generations of tomorrow. This long-term–relationship lens has to do with identity, grassroots (those people and relationships affected by harm), root causes, broken pasts, and shared futures.

Personal care-response is a relational orientation that calls us to care for particular people. A generations lens, as a virtue, expands that orientation to care for the past and the future.

The second virtue pair in this circle is transformation and humility. When transformation is a virtue, the goal is not just to fine-tune a basically working system but rather to seek to radically change people, systems, and dreams for the future. To encourage change toward justpeace is to move away from life-destroying ways of living toward life-nourishing ways of living.

Humility is about being aware of our limits. It is about respecting others, having an appropriate level of self-doubt, and not assuming that we know what others need. Humility lightens the spirit and creates the freedom to try, as the expectation is that we will not change everything. Humility has a sense of the possible, the complex, and the limits of our influence. It cultivates servant-based and facilitative leadership over expert leadership.

When transformation and humility are linked, change is sought through listening, empowering, and seeking a holistic vision.

In chapter 4 we explore the final circle: "The Creative Search for Truth." Here the virtues of needs orientation and nonviolence are held together in creative tension. For justpeace to be a lived experience, it must be oriented toward meeting the needs of all parties. Self-defined needs of victims, offenders, and communities must be central, not peripheral. Most conflict is rooted in unfulfilled needs. Justice is therefore about meeting needs, and in order to be needs oriented, its processes and ends must be flexible.

Justpeace requires that needs must be secured through nonviolent means. Nonviolence calls us to find nonviolent mechanisms for expressing and handling conflict. It favors cooperative methods such as circles and conferencing over adversarial ones such as the courts. The offense was not nonviolent, but neither is doing harm to the offender. And neither is the environment that created the conditions within which the offense took place. Needs-oriented nonviolence is concerned with all of these levels.

The final linked pair of virtues is empowerment and re-sponsibility. Empowerment recognizes that participants are not recipients of justpeace but rather resources of justpeace. Empowerment calls us to avoid imposing solutions from without and instead to involve all affected parties in meaning-ful participation. Empowerment creates space for the inclu-sion, participation, and voice of those affected by a conflict. Injustice robs people of power. Justpeace returns power.

Responsibility recognizes that as people gain power, they also gain responsibility to care for those around them. When interconnected relationships are harmed through con-flict or crime, responsibility increases. Responsibility calls us to change justice systems from a culture that discourages offenders from taking responsibility to one that encourages taking responsibility. Responsibility is about accountability to those affected by your decisions.

Each chapter provides examples of best practice. Each section ends with a set of questions designed to help cultivate these virtues. The questions explore how the virtues might in-fluence our visions of justpeace and our practices of conflict design, intervention, and evaluation. The goal is not to advocate specific models or methods of peacebuilding. Rather it is to expand our creative capacity to link with diverse contexts and to affirm and to cocreate experiences of beautiful, ethical, and strategic justpeace.

TWO

The Heart of the Matter:
Interconnectedness and Particularity

Interconnectedness
& Particularity

The inner circle addresses the question of the very nature of life. We examine the character of life, of justice and peace. From this point everything else ripples out. The questions at the end of the chapter try to help groups and individuals reflect on their best understanding of the nature of life.

If we believe life to be essentially violent, chaotic, and disordered, then we might imagine that we need a tough, violent justice to tame the evil world. This understanding has often been the approach taken from the time of the Reformation through the Enlightenment and modernity. We continue to see this approach in the rhetoric in our "tough-on-crime" campaigns and in the "war on terror." We also see this stream strongly coming from some faith-based groups. In some Christian circles, the focus on our essential and innate

sinfulness allows us to treat humans (and the rest of the natural world) as vile or, in the words of the famous Reformation
leader Martin Luther, as "totally depraved," "savage," and
"wild beasts."[1] Particular understandings of grace, faith, and
God sometimes lead toward a violent fight to tame the evil
world. The various forms of fundamentalism that have arisen
in many faith traditions often play with this imagination,
with this understanding of the true nature of life. But is that
the only alternative?

The peacebuilders I have studied had a different approach. They worked daily in contexts of violence, disruption,
and chaos, but they believed that life in its fullest sense had
very different essential qualities.

They believed that life is about relationships, beauty,
change, identity, and diversity. They believed that everything
that God created was indeed sacred, somehow reflecting the
very being of God—justice, righteousness, truth, love. They
also believed that we did not have to wait to die and get into
heaven before we could touch and taste these essential characteristics of life. When people forget how to reflect those
essential characteristics, the task of justpeace building is to
help them remember who they truly are. What makes the
approach of these peacebuilders interesting is that they did
not confine these "family values" to their family and friends,
to those who would love them in return. They believed the
same virtues could be applied very practically to the ever-
widening circles of self, family, friends, acquaintances, neighbors, strangers, and even enemies. Most approaches to justice
and peace assume that when we deal with these groups, we

1. Cited by Witte in "Between Sanctity and Depravity," 728.

need to suspend the normal everyday virtues of friendship, care, respect, and love. We suspend these virtues and rather try to use violence and the administering of pain to encourage people to change. However the justpeace ethic works differently.

Justpeace flows out of a different understanding of the nature of life. Rupert Ross, in his survey of Aboriginal justice in Canada, suggests that Aboriginal peoples work out of an ethic of original sanctity.[2] Similar attempts in Christianity can be found in some forms of liberation theology, Celtic theology, and ecotheology.[3] More and more people are reexamining ethics in light of the inherent sacredness and goodness of all creation. A different ethic emerges from different understandings of the essential nature of life.

In this chapter we examine two virtues that describe the essential characteristics of life from the standpoint of several such engaged justpeace builders.

INTERCONNECTEDNESS:
THE BEGINNING, MIDDLE, AND END

> Injustice anywhere is a threat to justice everywhere. We are caught in an inescapable network of mutuality, tied in a single garment of destiny. Whatever affects one directly affects all indirectly.[4]

> —*Martin Luther King Jr.*

2. Ross, *Dancing with a Ghost*, 189–211.

3. For liberation theology, see Boff, *Cry of the Earth*; for Celtic theology, see Newell, *Each Day & Each Night*; for ecotheology, see Hallman, *Ecotheology*.

4. King, "Letter from Birmingham Jail."

Life is relationship. All beauty and all suffering come from this reality. We live in a web of unfolding relationships. This is our "single garment of destiny" where every act has universal dimensions, where my liberty is connected to your liberty. One Aboriginal woman peacebuilder described these thick interconnection as the place "where the pain of one is the pain of all and where the harmony and joy of one is the harmony and joy of all."[5]

Different cultures and faith traditions have different terminology, all pointing toward the essential and sacred interconnectedness of the world: the Judeo-Christian understanding of shalom (right relationship with the earth, people, Creator, and self); the Buddhist understanding of dependent origin and inter being; the Mohawk Kaienerekowa (Great Law); the Greek understanding of Logos; the Hindu understanding of ahimsa; the Australian Aborigine understanding of Songlines; or the Christian understanding of Christ, in whom all things made hold together (Col 1:15–17). Behind each of these wisdom traditions is an understanding of a deeply interconnected and interdependent world. Everything else ripples out from this vision. Recognition of the sacredness of the other is at the core of this virtue.

Even the new sciences are recognizing the interconnected and changing nature of the world. From the science of quantum physics to that of global warming, we see new understandings of the essential interconnectedness of our world.

Yet most of us have been raised with a different understanding of the world. We have been taught that the world

5. Thakur, *Circles*.

is chaotic, violent, and dangerous. We have been taught that we are in a struggle to impose order where only the fittest survive. We have been taught that to be free is to be an autonomous individual, independent of all foreign influences. Individualism, materialism, and capitalism have led us to view life as a fight to extract and secure resources for "me and my kind"—at anyone's expense. This perverse vision clouds our thinking.

In this view, justice is imposed from the top down, dealing out punishment and pain in the futile hope of taming an essentially violent world. Again, the implications of this vision are profound. From state violence that is legally sanctioned to interpersonal violence that is not, from structural violence that systematizes the unjust order to violent revolutions that try to lift the order, we hold a common vision of a chaotic world where the path to justice involves the same cruel behavior we wish to stop—the unilateral imposition of my will over yours. This is the logic of both the criminal and the criminal courts. Not surprisingly, this kind of hierarchical justice is rarely healing.

In this dominant worldview, the way to truth is through dividing up and breaking apart, and through adversaries conflicting. It is also the logic of our approaches to health, education, and sometimes even spirituality. We divide up the world into many little boxes, be it through a personal day-timer or through an organizational structure kept in such places as prisons, schools, or hospitals. We even divide the world in our thinking through various dualism and dichotomies: subject/object, them/us, oppressed/oppressor, private/public, either/or. We believe that by taking things apart, we can get to what is truly essential. However, we are often just left with many broken pieces.

We have become better at taking apart than at putting back together, better at defending our territory than at meeting the needs of the other, better at assessing blame than at making things right, better at creating knowledge than at creating wisdom, better at ruling over than living alongside, better at breaking than healing. In our search for truth, we discover many facts but unveil little meaning. For too many, the search for truth and justice is a process of losing their own identity and their capacity to taste and see the fullness of life.

Justpeace ethics begins with a vision of an interconnected, relationship-centered world. The beginning and the end of justpeace is a vision of community. It is a vision of beautiful right relationship. Martin Luther King Jr. called it the "beloved community." Hear his poignant words: "The aftermath of *nonviolence* is the creation of the beloved community, while the aftermath of violence is tragic bitterness."[6] Howard Zehr's classic text on restorative justice, *Changing Lenses*, describes a biblical justice rooted in such a vision of interconnectedness, or shalom.[7] With this imagination, Zehr sees penetratingly through the current system and orients us toward a kind of justice based on respect and common connection rather than on disrespect and isolation.

Interconnectedness is both the end goal and the means to get there. What we strive for in every step of the path is not primarily about ending conflict, that is, cutting off or resolving conflicted relationships, but about building a peaceful beloved community. It is a holistic ecological vision of liv-

6. King, "Nonviolence and Racial Justice," 8.
7. Zehr, *Changing Lenses*, 126–57.

ing full and joyful lives where all the many seen and unseen relationships continue in symbiotic balance, where we are encouraged, enabled, and compelled to become part of the creative, liberating, and communal song of creation. This is the end goal and also the means.

As a category of conflict analysis, the virtue of interconnectedness shows us that injustice is broken relationships. While noting the substance of a conflict, we would give primary attention to tracking the people and relationships involved. It is through becoming mindful of these that we are able to enter meaningfully into the tangled web of relationships and to help engage transformation.

As an intervention strategy, interconnectedness leads us to work collaboratively across conflict lines rather than dividing between conflicting parties (defense/prosecution, them/us). It focuses on building relational networks and connecting with the community of people already engaged in the context. It focuses on creating a multiplicity of strategies alongside local people rather than a single-track strategy run by outside experts.

When our evaluation focuses on how well we are doing with regard to the virtue of interconnectedness, we move away from linear approaches of adding up inputs to achieve certain outcomes. Outcome-based evaluation may work well in fixed environments but often falls short in environments of ongoing changing relationships. It limits our vision to our current perspective. Our goal in evaluation of the interconnectedness perspective is to increase our capacity to learn about our relationships and about how change happens. Evaluation is about entering into the web of relationships and learning how to be present in ways that lead to beauty for all. To some people, the goal to work for beauty for all will be seen as naïve and idealistic. Perhaps it is rare, but such sentiment does have some precedent in the Hebrew Bible. Moses is instructed to cultivate a community capable of responding to harms in such a way that all go home in shalom, in right relationship with God, land, self, and stranger (Exod 18:13–23). Here we see the need to cultivate means of conflict intervention that create peace across diverse sets of interconnected relationships so that all go home in peace.

From the perspective of interconnectedness, context, relationships, history, social structures, and systems may all be relevant factors when harm is committed. However, these factors may not be used as excuses not to address the direct harm or its victim. These must be addressed if justice is to be experienced fully. The virtue of interconnectedness calls us to deal with both the case issues and the larger systemic issues.

Aboriginal justice circles demonstrate the virtue of interconnectedness. The facilitators gather people with various connections to the victim, offender, and others affected by harm. They first address the obligations to the victim and, second, the interconnected relationships that caused the offender to harm a relationship in the first place.[8] When the circle includes not just victim and offender but family and a broad cross-section of the community, new opportunities for justpeace building emerge. In Aboriginal contexts, this larger circle does not respond just to the incident, episode, or presenting symptom. It digs at deeper issues of identity, peoplehood, connection, patterns of behavior, ways the community and the surrounding systems may have contributed to the harm, and ways they might contribute to harmony and wholeness.

8. Pranis et al., *Peacemaking Circles*; Canada, *Four Circles*.

Interconnectedness is a vision of reality. Our task as peacebuilders and justice workers is to root our project conception, intervention, and evaluation in the very character of life. The following questions are designed to help us think concretely of the virtue of interconnectedness in various conflict settings.

Ethically Guiding Questions Rooted in *Interconnection*:

Eliciting Vision Questions: We would do well to examine our own traditions to see what they teach about the nature of life. Is life essentially violent or essentially a sacred gift? Is it something else entirely? Where are the resources that teach about interconnection, beauty, and the fullness of life? Where are the resources which teach about the essentially violent nature of life?

Design/Analysis Questions: How do you respect and create space for many and different voices? How do you connect with and strengthen existing peacebuilding initiatives?

Intervention Questions: Does this program move you toward a shared interdependent future where peace and justice coexist? Does the intervention consider the social, systemic, ecological, spiritual, and personal implications?

Evaluation Questions: How is the program being received by those doing similar work? What are the unintended consequences? Does the program help people to find their way back to a balanced life?

PARTICULARITY:
THE ROOTS AND FLAVOR BUDS OF JUSTPEACE

Taste and see that the LORD is good.

—Psalm 34:8

The fullness of life is meant to be tasted, seen, and touched. This justice is not bitter or sour or ugly. When we draw from the rich diversity of particularity, we learn that justice is a rich feast, a good, satisfying, beautiful feast. Particularity forms the roots and the flavor buds of justpeace. By "roots," I mean the capacity to draw out or absorb from the surrounding environment that which is needed for life. By "flavor buds," I mean those almost invisible qualities that allow us to appreciate the texture, spice, and temperature of the experiences we need for a full life. As with interconnectedness, the beginning and ending of justpeace finds its place in particularity.

Particularity is about valuing particular identity. Whereas interconnectedness examines the relationships between all elements, particularity examines the particular identity of each element. Whereas interconnectedness draws on our commonness, particularity highlights our distinctiveness and difference.

Western culture generally values universality over particularity. Universality says that we are essentially the same, have the same needs, and need the same access to power and resource and even the same methods, in order to become fully human. In fact, universality tries to reduce our many particular stories into one universal human story. The blindfolded Lady Justice, with scales to measure out sameness and a sword to make it painful, aptly illustrates this sense of universal justice. To ignore the identity of those before you (as indicated by the blindfold on Lady Justice) and to dish out equal amounts of pain is the iconic picture of ugly justice. And yet the empirical evidence is very clear. Universal processes do not liberate; they oppress. They impose on people and pressure them to lose their own identity and assimilate to the dominant culture. This is a dominator's sense of justice. The disproportionate number of, on the one hand, African

Americans in U.S. jails and, on the other hand, First Nations people in Canadian jails demonstrates the racist tendency and deep failure of universal justice systems.

Sometimes those in the fields of conflict transformation and restorative justice criticize the "universal" state system of justice only to advocate replacing it with another single-track process, the mediation process or Victim Offender Conferencing. Yet this change is still inspired by the hope of the old imagination: "if we could just find one good process, everything will work out okay." Not true.

Particularity takes us down a different path. Particularity says that the identity, culture, and context of those involved in harms and healing must be a central source for understanding and intervening in all conflicts. Rather than beginning with a process like mediation, courts, or war, and trying to apply it to all situations, particularity begins with the situations, with the people involved, and with their cultures and contexts. It begins by claiming and building on the understandings and capacities of the local community.

Particularity trusts that there are already resources in place locally that have the capacity to enter respectfully and transformatively into this situation. State justice tends to take conflicts away from communities and thereby weakens them. Even now although some areas of justice are being returned to communities, state rules often impose impartial expert inter-veners or judicially supervised agreements.[9] Thus the virtue of local resources, of particularity, is severely limited. Blind Lady Justice stands where elders and community circles once stood. When the particular identity of peoples is respected,

9. United Nations Economic and Social Council, *Basic Principles*.

they are freed to determine for themselves who would best facilitate an intervention or supervise an agreement or even determine if interventions and agreements are really what are needed. A foreign process (the law) and an outcome that removes people from their roots and relations (prisons) might not be the wisest strategy.

Particularity sees the world as diverse. Justice is not seen as some abstract, distant principle but rather something that is experienced, or tasted, in relationships. Those relationships, together with the context and the culture in which they are set, need to be central for justice to be experienced.

One example of this particularity comes from Family Group Conferences (FGC) in New Zealand.[10] In the 1980s New Zealanders went through a long process of wrestling with how their justice and social-service systems were institutionally racist toward the indigenous Maori people, and not all that effective for the Pekah (white) people either. Their first step was to change how they approached harmful behavior in young people. They shelved their previous youth criminal-justice legislation, and in 1989 introduced the Young Persons and Their Families Act. This act laid out principles of the FGC. To some degree, this act tried to build on a Maori understanding of harm, namely, that in responding to harm, the family must be strengthened at every step. But the act did not proclaim FGC as preset technique or process. Although many treated FGC in this style, the original vision was that FGCs were a principled vessel, which the youth worker needs to fill with the relevant people, places, and questions appropriate to the context. According to New Zealand law, Family Group

10. MacRae and Zehr, *Little Book of Family Group Conference.*

Conferencing is not a process but a set of principles. Every FGC in New Zealand looks different, depending on the context and ethnoreligious identity of the people involved in the harm. This should be the case with all peacebuilding actions.

Scripted, rigid processes do not give space for the role of particularity of identity or culture. Particularity demands space for flexibility and creativity. Justpeace is not imposed but is created alongside those most intimately involved in the harm. One of the critical tasks of any life-giving initiative is to resist being co-opted, universalized, and overstructured. When a flower gets plucked from its roots, it will die. The Australian police noticed the success New Zealand was having with youth crime and decided to introduce Family Group Conferencing as a tool of state control. They took something that was to be flexible and made it rigid and scripted. They took something that was meant to liberate the country from systemic racism and used it to further state control. They took something that was meant to strengthen extended families and used it as a rationale for uniformed police officers shaming children. Before the Australian model failed and was discarded, Canada imposed Family Group Conferencing (Australian-style). The introduction of Family Group Conferencing to Australia and Canada are two examples of just how quickly we overlook the virtue of particularity. A creative way of responding to harms that drew on local Maori culture in New Zealand became an instrument of state control when imposed from the top down with a very uncreative script and very little local connection. Peacebuilders and justice workers should be suspicious of any prepackaged foreign method to deal with conflict. While there is much we can learn from others, the journey of justpeace is the path to rediscovering our place and our identity in this world. Imposing foreign understandings rarely leads to such a rediscovery.

Peacebuilders should rather develop culturally contextualized, elicitive approaches that draw upon concepts in the local culture.[11] Particularity recognizes that conflicts are the property of particular communities, not states or professionals.[12] Rather than focusing on the role of an external facilitator/intervener, we should work to facilitate the emergence of peacebuilders and an infrastructure for peace within the conflict setting (elders, family, and community). To do this will require great courage and trust. We will have to let go of the basic assumption that any one method of decision making (even democracy) is good for all situations. We will have to trust that creating space for difference that is rooted in authentic identity will lead to a more fruitful life.

From the standpoint of particularity, stability comes from complexity and diversity more than from uniformity. Valuing particularity is about creating space for diverse complexity where many particular identities are all connected and interacting. Through this lens, monoculture and the globalization of culture are seen as more of a threat to global stability than a help. Life flourishes in its fullness: not when we become like robots, mechanistic and all the same, but when we learn to be fully distinct and fully connected.

The psalmist, who dares us to "taste and see that the Lord is good," also tells us to "look to [God] and be radiant; so your faces shall never be ashamed" (Ps 34:5). Here is an understanding that the true nature of life is good and can be tasted and seen in this world. The good understanding of

11. Lederach, *Preparing for Peace*.

12. Christie, "Conflict as Property."

life is reinforced by the admonition that we are to be radiant rather than ashamed. The path of justpeace is one that moves from shame to radiance, from fear of a violent world to participation in the sacredness of this world.

Ethically Guiding Questions Rooted in *Particularity*:

Eliciting Vision Questions: What are the resources in your tradition for respecting difference, dissonance, and disruption? What are the practices for loving each individual? What are the reminders in your tradition to let things take root where they are so that they can bloom beautifully?

Design/Analysis Questions: Is the analysis and design coming from the perspective of those involved in the conflict? What are the natural and healthy ways by which a conflict gets dealt with in that context? Are victims given space to articulate their own experience of harms and healing?

Intervention Questions: Are there respected people within the setting who are or could be facilitating intervention? Are you creating space for identity searching and forming? Does this intervention impose outside ways of dealing with conflict, or does it build internal resources? Is this intervention rooted in local cultural and/or spiritual resources?

Evaluation Questions: What was learned about what worked well with that particular group, context, and time? What local infrastructure could be enhanced to build toward long-term justpeace? What is being learned about the local vision of justpeace, and how could this understanding change future conflict interaction?

SUMMARY: HOLDING TOGETHER
INTERCONNECTEDNESS AND PARTICULARITY

Interconnectedness says that we are connected, and that harms create responsibilities to those most affected (victims, community, family). Particularity adds that while we are connected, we are not all the same. Justpeace must respect both our connections and our particularity.

This is the most basic ethical tension in life. How can I be fully true to who I am (particularity) while at the same time fully and respectfully connected to others (interconnectedness)? The intersecting point of this quest is finding meaningful belonging and respectful coexistence in community. This type of belonging is precisely what is lost for victim and offender when the ripples of unjust harms shatter relationships, community, identity, and meaning. This is what justpeace seeks to restore.

I have sometimes heard Aboriginal people speak of how planting corn, beans, and squash together in one hill leads to healthier plants than growing them apart. Aboriginal people say that people and communities are meant to be like that: each plant helps the other to grow—distinct yet interdependent. This is a beautiful picture of balancing our particularity and our interconnectedness.

THREE

A Relational-Focused Approach to Change

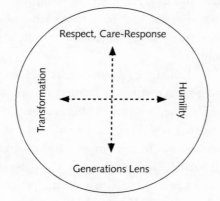

This second circle of virtues begins with the question of *who* and extends to the question of *change*. When reality is seen in its vast interconnectedness, and each element is respected (particularity), the question of identity quickly rises to the surface. Who am I? Who are we? How do we relate to "them"? What will become of "us"? Peacebuilding that is rooted in interconnected relationships begins with these questions of *who*: Who is connected to this harm or healing or both? What is the nature of these unfolding relationships? Who has capacity to spark change? These questions are prior to questions of *what*.[1] Questions of *what* tend to focus on issues rather

1. Lederach, *Building Peace*.

than relationships. What issues need to be resolved? What agreements could be put in place? What needs to be done to make things right? Often the "*what* issues" are symptoms of deeper problems embedded in the structure of relationships, relationships that need attention before we can focus only on issues and solutions. By focusing first on the relational dynamics, justpeace ethics deepens the analysis and surfaces more of the driving energy behind conflict and behind efforts at justice and peacebuilding. Through examining the virtues of care-response and generations lens, we will bring into focus this relationship-centered approach to change in peacebuilding.

Chris Marshall argues that this relational focus is actually "one of the most distinctive features of biblical teaching on justice and righteousness."[2] As biblical justice is really a collective and covenantal justice, we can see a strong sense of justice worked out in the context and commitments of the parties involved. This relational focus contrasts with approaches that focus more narrowly on the private, the individual, and the abstract. This kind of justpeace gets worked out in the context of relationships.

The virtues of transformation and humility will guide us into the complexity and richness of ongoing, unfolding change. As anyone involved in relationships knows, to enter a relationship is to enter shifting ground. Healthy relationships are dynamic, beautiful, and surprising because they do not stay the same. Even unhealthy relationships do not stay the same. To be in unfolding relationships is to be in unfolding change. This chapter reflects on a relationship-centered approach to change.

2. Marshall, *Biblical Justice*, 35.

CARE-RESPONSE AND GENERATIONS-LENS VIRTUES

Care-Response: Respecting People

> According to my experience, the principle charac-
> teristic of genuine happiness is peace: inner peace.
> . . . The peace I am describing is rooted in concern
> for others. . . . I attribute my sense of peace to the
> effort to develop concern for others.[3]

> —*Dalai Lama*

When justice gets co-opted, we lose sight of these basic insights that justice and peace are about care for and with real people. Too often we cast aside both the victim and the offender. We ignore the communities and the identities of the people most intimately affected by harm. We make justice into an institution, into a set of rules, or into a set of rights. Likewise we make peace into a settlement or accord between high-level leaders, often losing sight of the grassroots. Harms are no longer seen as offenses between people but become violations of rules or rights, offenses against the state. Countries are not seen for the people they comprise but rather the potential resources or threats they hold for power-hungry nations competing for scarce resources. We hide the victims and substitute institutions. Within these institutions, our adversarial search for facts destroys relationships. We create winners and losers but lose community and collective identity. Sometimes these state forms of justice and peace-building destroy the very people who need to struggle with justpeace to make them strong.

Justpeace ethics recovers the central place of relationship to self, community, and "the other" in justice. Kay Harris's

3. Dalai Lama XIV, *Ethics for the New Millennium*, 57–58.

"Moving into the New Millennium: Toward a Feminist Vision of Justice" speaks of this shift as a shift from a rules/rights response to a care-response.[4] It begins by gathering the people most affected by harm, and it tries to create a caring space that might lead to healing and wholeness. It is about sharing in the sufferings of others, not from the perspective of piety or cheap charity but from the vantage point of deep respect. Howard Zehr makes a similar argument. As injustice is so often about losing respect, whether for victim, for offender, or for community, a justice that heals needs to be about giving respect.[5]

For many people, conflict is the process of losing oneself. Whether it is the conflict of being a victim of a traumatizing event or the conflict of being one who victimizes others, or even the conflict of the bystander who passively watches as someone else loses their humanity: in each case we lose something of our own humanity, something of our identity. Aboriginal people often say of such a person, "She has forgotten who she is." That is to say, if we are truly grounded in our identity (our cultural, spiritual, ethnic, ecological and human identity), then the healing path is readily available to us. Victims, offenders, and communities all need caring spaces to rediscover who they are and how to live in right relationship. Rather than blaming or ignoring those whom we don't understand (the victims), we would do well to listen deeply and transformatively to their stories. Rather than dehumanize those we see as our enemies (as is the policy of our justice system, of our military strategy, of our foreign-affairs departments, and even to some extent of our medical system), we

4. Harris, "Moving into the New Millennium," 83–97.
5. See Zehr, "Justice That Heals: The Vision."

need to learn creative ways of holding people responsible in such a way that they regain their humanity.

This is not a soft, avoidance approach to justice. It is rooted in the hope and the belief that a caring response is more powerful and more healing than punishment in getting through to victims, offenders, and communities. Victim Offender Conferencing (VOC) is one way of responding to harms by keeping care for real people central. While the justice system largely ignores victims and offenders, VOC sees these people as primary participants in experiencing justice. By creating a space for offenders both to voice their experience directly to the person whom they have harmed and to take responsibility for their behavior, VOC creates opportunities for caring and healing.[6] In confronting harms, care-response searches for responses that care for real people and relationships, especially the victims, offenders and communities.

Care, love, compassion—these cannot be legislated, and they cannot be done (lived out) by an institution. The Bible calls us to love the self, the neighbor, the alien, and even the enemy. When Israel neglected these tasks, the prophets named this behavior injustice and oppression. Ivan Illich's reflection in *The Corruption of Christianity* touches on precisely this point.[7] He dates the beginning of the corruption of Christianity back to the fourth century when Christianity became a state religion. One of the first changes was that the hospitality to the stranger was taken out of the homes of Christians and made into a state institution—the beginning of our welfare system. That which was relational was made institutional. That which was dynamic was made static. That which

6. Umbreit, *Handbook of Victim Offender Meditation*; Zehr, *Changing Lenses*.

7. Illich and Cayley, *Corruption of Christianity*

was uplifting was made oppressive. The same is true for our modern justice system. That which belongs in the realm of loving interaction between people becomes institutionalized, bureaucratic, foreign, and oppressive. When care-response is a virtue, institutionalization must always be resisted.

When some method works well, our tendency is to package it, make into a formula, and use it universally. This approach, however, does not give sufficient space to either our particularity or our need to care and be cared for. Care-response reminds us that justice is a quality of interaction in relationships.

Ethically Guiding Questions Rooted in *Care-Response*:

Eliciting Vision Questions: How does your tradition remind people to care for the stranger? The alien? The enemy? The self? How can do you nurture care as a quality between people rather than as a task of institutions? Whose responsibility is it to care? What is expected of such people?

Design/Analysis Questions: Are participants part of the design process? What relationships have been affected by this harm? Whose responsibility are these harms? How can all participants be treated with respect at every stage of the process?

Intervention Questions: Does the intervention help parties to see each other as human and help them toward working out care and response for each other? Is support offered to help participants understand the experience and needs of the other? How can circles of care and support be set up for those involved in this harm?

Evaluation Questions: Did participants feel that they experienced justice, care, and peace? Were participants given ample opportunity to learn to care for each other? What new opportunities are arising where we could build a relational network?

The Generations Lens—Expanding Time

> The only way we can survive is to recover our strength, our wisdom, and our solidarity by honoring and revitalizing the core of our traditional teachings. Only by heeding the voice of our ancestors can we restore our nations and put peace, power and righteousness back into the hearts and minds of our people.[8]
>
> —*Taiaiake Alfred*

A generations lens is a relational virtue with a long-term time dimension. The generations lens is not just concerned with people currently affected by a conflict but also with those who have gone before and those who will come after. A generations lens looks both to the past and to the future to determine the best way to relate to the present. A generations lens becomes a virtue when it shapes our perspectives. It has to do with identity, grassroots, root causes, broken pasts, and shared futures. The good news and the bad news is that broadening the time dimensions offers many more resources (e.g., traditional teachings) while at the same time expanding the scope of relationships that need to be healed.

Without a generations lens, we might act only out of our self-interest and thereby undermine the quality of life of future generations. We might get caught in the cycle of crisis after crisis, or worse yet, we might lose our whole sense of history and identity. When in conflict, we often need to return to the point where our story was most interrupted to create meaning and address fundamental identity questions. This kind of generations lens seeks taking of not just indi-

8. Alfred, *Peace, Power, Righteousness*, xii.

vidual responsibility but also taking of collective responsibility and perhaps even collective atonement making. Often this involves returning to the wisdom of the ancestors to relearn who we are and how we are to be in this world. Too often peacebuilders give space only to present dynamics and future hopes, thereby cutting people off from both the pain and the resources of their roots.

Among the Mohawks, a chief is called to use the principle of seven generations when making important decisions. The problems of today are in part the result of decisions made seven generations ago. The decision made today will affect children seven generations to come. In this wide horizon of time, issues of land, spirit, collective and common survival come to the fore. Unlike democracy, which typically works on four to five year spans of time, this long generational lens seeks not just personal political power but sustainable patterns of relationship with land, neighbor, and enemy. Going back in time creates space to move fruitfully into the future.

When the generations lens expands our timeframe of awareness, we no longer see just the current harm. We begin to see the systems, structures and patterns in which the harm is embedded. The generations lens is not satisfied with a case focus unconnected to system change. One of the critical issues in restorative justice is to learn to move beyond case orientation to issues of systemic change. Often case-oriented resolution of conflict strengthens the status quo. By decreasing work conflicts, the business can run more smoothly. This is a wise and beneficial strategy if you believe in the status quo. But what if you don't? The generations lens is a somewhat subversive lens. It has the memory that things have not always been the way they are now. It is not satisfied with pulling people out of the river (a short-term crisis response). It digs deeper to see why they are being thrown into the river in the first place.

Until we work at healing the whole community and the many ways its members interconnect, social problems will continue to abound. Even if we could end conflict and crisis we would not yet be on the road to the fullness of life. We would just be a void. If we want harmonious, balanced, just relationships for our children and grandchildren, then we must start building them and living them now. Martin Luther King's "I Have a Dream" speech worked because it drew on just such a generational perspective. He speaks of his future dreams for his grandchildren. His dream for the future generations is shaped by a careful understanding of the past generations, going back to biblical stories. But he speaks of them in this manner so as to open up a new way of being in the present, one that embodies the generational vision and that disturbs the present structures. For King, this way of being in the present came through nonviolent direct action. The generations lens seeks not just to address harms as they arise but seeks also to educate and empower people to live in harmonious ways that do not cause harms in the first place.

It is this generations lens that helped the First Nations People at Hollow Water in Manitoba, Canada, to address patterns of sexual abuse through restorative means. Hollow Water realized they had an 80 percent sexual-abuse rate going back several generations. The individual guilt-punishment justice system was not helping to stop the problem. They decided to take a generational approach to stopping harm and cultivating the good life.[9] Part of what was recognized in

9. Canada, *Four Circles of Hollow Water*.

Hollow Water is that the pain of abuse and neglect is passed down through the generations. The Community Holistic Circle Healing approach that they developed was rated many times more fruitful than any other sexual-abuse strategy in Canada.[10]

One need only to look back three or four generations in your own family to see how pain and trauma gets transmitted. As much as those of us in individualistic cultures wish to believe that we are completely independent, we are not. We are because others are. We are because of those who have gone before. We are because of those who are around us. This affects everything from the healing of trauma to international economics, from who we are to who they are. So if pain flows very freely through the generations, so too can justpeace. The generations lens heightens our awareness of our power to learn from generations gone by and to transform generations yet to come. For good or for bad, we will influence the generations yet to come.

This generations lens has to do with the life of a people. With this in mind, an impartial, external conflict facilitator might be exactly the wrong approach. When we look at a whole person and at the whole context of his or her people, we begin to see that many *in situ* people may have more capacity to lead justpeace processes than an off-site person. I heard a young man from Northwest Territories in Canada say it this way: "When judges sentence you, you never see them. When elders sentence, the next day you go to the Northern Store and get the mail and there standing in line with you are all the judges." We don't all have respected elders, but we

10. Couture, "Cost-Benefit Analysis."

are connected to a multitude of people. Creating space for traditional leaders and for extended families can help us to draw on the resources of the generations-lens virtue.

Ethically Guiding Questions Rooted in *Generations Lens*:

Eliciting Vision Questions: Where are the best sources within your tradition for looking through a "generations lens," looking both to the past and to the future? In your tradition, what comes into focus as the lens extends through the generations? What are the new horizons of peace and justice? What are the new horizons of suffering and oppression?

Design/Analysis Questions: Who should be analyzing and designing this process? Are there family/clan members who can help? What are the root causes of this current conflict? Are there decisions that were made generations ago that are affecting these current events? Is there structural conflict (something in the way that we organize ourselves) fueling this conflict? What would be best for the children several generations in the future?

Intervention Questions: Are families being strengthened? How do you minimize harm that might be passed on to future generations? How does one ensure and maximize justpeace getting passed on to future generations? Who is leading the process?

Evaluation Questions: What are the intended and unintended effects on generations to come? Does this program have the capacity to transform the status quo when needed? Could that capacity be enhanced by viewing through the "generations lens"?

Holding Together Care-Response *and the* Generations Lens

Both care-response and the generations lens virtues have to do with relationships and real people. The virtue of care/response can be seen to be biased toward the present. The generations lens expands this by underlining the moral quality of time, extending into both the past and the future. When the personal and the generational are linked, people and their current actions are linked to the generations of both the past and the future, including their visions. We must relate to people today in the way we would like to see the world in fifty years. This is the ethical mandate of justpeace.

TRANSFORMATION AND HUMILITY

Transformation—The Status Quo Is Not Okay

> Education either functions as an instrument which is used to facilitate integration of the younger generation into the logic of the present system and bring about conformity or it becomes "the practice of freedom," the means by which men and women deal critically and creatively with reality and discover how to participate in the transformation of their world.[11]
>
> —*Richard Shaull*

Transformation is the belief and the hope that we are not held captive to our present system. This virtue seeks to destabilize those imposed, settled, static states of peace and justice.[12] The *Pax Romana* (the peace of the Romans from about 27 BCE to 180 CE) sought a peace that comes from empire building. That peace was imposed, settled, and maintained by a mix of diplomacy, structural adjustment, and violence. But the "Pax Christi," or peace of Christ, is different. Jesus embodied a way of peace and change that was seen as a threat to the empire builders and to the religious establishment. Yet it is this kind

11. Freire, *Pedagogy of the Oppressed*, 34.
12. Huebner, *Precarious Peace*.

of radical transformation that justpeace ethics tries to nurture. It does not seek to maintain the state but to cultivate the practice of healing. It is the belief that healing change is possible, desirable, natural, and accessible. Transformation is the courage to address our brokenness, to work at what we need to do in order to come together and to restore the sacred interconnections of life.

Victims, offenders, communities, nations, even institutions can change. Life wants to heal. If you cut your skin, it soon heals. If we pour chemicals on the earth, eventually, if left alone, the earth heals. If we try to commit genocide against a whole people, eventually they will rise up. Life is resilient despite our best efforts to destroy it. Our challenge is to find creative ways to join in this healing, this resilient impulse, and to avoid those ways that thwart it.

One of the biggest obstacles to healing transformation is the ease with which we write it off as impossible: "Restorative justice is good for petty crime but not for violent, repeat offenders. They are beyond change."

"*Nonviolence* might work on good people but not on evil dictators and terrorists."

"Telling the truth is good for kindergarten children but is impractical for politicians."

"Friendship is good for those close to you but is not a sound basis for international relations."

We are quick to believe that the realm of the good is very small and that everything else is violent and dangerous and must be dealt with in violent, dangerous, and terror-ful ways.

Transformation believes that healing is possible and comes through transforming relationships. What relation-

ships? Our identity (particularity), our place in the web of relationships that we call life (interconnectedness), our capacity
to care for others (care-response), and the systems and structures in which we relate (generations lens). All these relationships are open to be transformed. Transformation calls us to
learn who we are and how we are connected to the world, and
then to engage compassionately with all of life.

This type of deep transformation takes time and requires
patience. It focuses on lives of people and on how they deal
with day-to-day harm and healing over the long term. It is not
interested in cheap peace through a shortsighted crime policy
such as incarceration, which sometimes increases crime, or in
quick restitution agreements that leave participants broken
and unable to heal. Neither is this transformation primarily concerned with high-profile peace accords that do little
to transform the life of the grass roots. Deep transformation
seeks to transform unjust relationships into relationships of
justice and peace that draw deeply from diverse and particular contexts.

This transformation is not the realm of experts, scholars,
and others who are far off. This transformation is accessible
to everyone. Our choices do make a difference. How we relate
to others in all aspects of life (our buying, our fuel consump-
tion, our communicating, and so on) does make a difference
for people around the world. This transformation does not
come from waiting for politicians to achieve it. It comes from
ordinary people deciding to participate in the transformation
of their world. Ironically, it seems that those who have been
most broken by life, and who are in the process of healing,
are the ones most aware of their capacity to participate in the
transformation of the world. It is not the strong and powerful

who are the engines of this transformation. It is the broken, the fragile, and the ones who are in the process of healing who are giving life to this change.

Transformation is biased. It is biased in the direction of justpeace. It is partial towards life-giving ways. It discriminates against life-destroying ways. It is not silent or neutral, neither is it oppressive or domineering. It is ready to engage, to come alongside, with love and care and deep respect for all. This transformation names particular kinds of moral imagination that draw us into the art and soul of peacebuilding.[13]

The Torah (biblical law) has a pedagogical or an educational function.[14] The goal is to point toward a kind of transformation. The goal of this biblical law is not procedural directions for lawyers. The transformative focus is the daily habits of all people. This transformation is less focused on regime change and more focused on what philosopher Michael de Certeau calls "the practice of everyday life,"[15] and what Buddhist peacebuilder Thich Nhat Hanh calls "peace in every step: the path of mindfulness in everyday life."[16]

John Paul Lederach defines this transformational capacity as the ability to "envision and respond to the ebb and flow of social conflict as life-giving opportunities for creative constructive change processes that reduce violence, increase justice in direct interaction and social structures in human relationships."[17]

13. Lederach, *Moral Imagination*.
14. Marshall, *Biblical Justice*, 15.
15. Certeau, *Practice of Everyday Life*.
16. Hanh, *Peace Is Every Step*.
17. Lederach, *Little Book of Conflict Transformation*, 14.

So how do we create space for the deep transformation of people, systems, and dreams? What does this mean for those who are embroiled in conflict?

Ethically Guiding Questions Rooted in *Transformation*:

Eliciting Vision Questions: How does your tradition practice change? How does change happen? What is being transformed? What are the sources of hope that transformation might be possible?

Design/Analysis Questions: How are people already responding to change and conflict in constructive ways, and how can this be enhanced? What do the poets, the dreamers, the visionaries say about justice and peace, and how can they be further engaged in constructive change processes? How are economic, political, and social structures connected with the current harm?

Intervention Questions: What change processes have the capacity to reduce violence and to increase justice? How can space be created for constructive direct interaction between parties in conflict?

Evaluation Questions: What is being learned about how constructive change happens? How can these new insights change current structures, relationships, and future interventions? What new meaning is being drawn out to help transcend this past brokenness?

Humility—The Only Restorative Attitude to Dealing with People and Complex Systems

> It is a wholesome and necessary thing for us to turn again to the earth and in the contemplation of her beauties to know the sense of wonder and humility.
>
> —*Rachel Carson*

There is a form of humility that leads to paralysis. It is a false humility that consumes the self: "I'm not good enough. I really don't have anything to offer here. There are plenty of people who could do this better than me."

This false humility consumes the soul with self-absorbed navel gazing, stripping the person of any ability to engage in fruitful transformation. This is not the type of humility advocated here.

The type of humility that inspires practitioners of peace and justice is the humility rooted in a deep respect for a world with a myriad interconnections. As biologist and environmentalist Rachel Carson suggests, something wonderful and absolutely vital is gained by allowing ourselves to enter into the beautiful mystery of the earth. Somehow in the vast otherness of creation we find ourselves again. We find our place, our spirit, and our longing for harmony. In this beautiful mystery we learn to walk lightly, to treat others with respect, and to be mindful of our own limitations.

Many traditional Aboriginal approaches to working with offenders include a time "on the land." This activity is exactly the type of humble contemplation that Rachel Carson suggests: to enter the wilderness to rediscover who we are. Aboriginal "on-the-land" programs are sometimes culture camps and sometimes simply time in the wilderness with an elder. But the goal remains the same: to break out of self-absorption and to rediscover who we are within this vast, interconnected world. This is the kind of humility of spirit characteristic of those who are on healing journeys.

The earth is not the only place where we can rediscover humility. Entering into the confusion and pain of deep harms quickly leads an honest person to humility. Touching the vulnerability of pain, we realize that we are treading on holy ground. Recognizing our own inability to see clearly, we begin the process of self-doubt. In conflict, our well-intended actions often have unintended consequences. In our attempt at creating ripples of justpeace, we sometimes create ripples of further injustice. What we thought would be an experience of liberation becomes an experience of oppression. What we thought might be a spark of change gets drowned in the river of momentum. Humility is the ability to admit our mistakes while at the same time staying at the table.

In the Christian Scriptures, we are told the reign of Jesus does not come by his having dominion over others but by his serving others and by humbling himself. Followers of Jesus are invited to interact with the world with the same imagination or self-understanding that Jesus had (Phil 2:5–8). Obviously some people use these stories like a sword—ready to kill and to cut out that which they see as not belonging. But the call is to a different way of engaging the world, a way that only comes through humility.

Once we make friends with humility, we can rediscover our capacity for playful tinkering.[18] Once we recognize the complexity of change and relationship, we are freed from the pressure of trying to find the one piece that is going to make all the difference. There is no "one piece that makes all the difference." There are multiple reasons why things are the way they are. There are multiple actions that are needed to change this current dynamic constructively. This complexity can be overwhelming. And indeed if we are primarily motivated by guilt or pride or fear, we will likely be quickly overwhelmed. However, when immersed in humility, we develop a strategic ability to see and a gently playful capacity to act.

When we are freed to doubt even our own actions, we can begin to see the larger system. Freed from the need to prove that our actions are working, we become open to the

18. Wheatley and Kellner-Rogers, *Simpler Way*.

possibility that our actions could be fueling larger, more systemic injustice. Our effort to calm a racial dispute (a case focus) may in fact be contrary to our larger goal as it enables an unjust system to keep working. Humble conflict analysis recognizes that there is a lot of stuff going on that we can't see.

Yet humility is one of the first qualities to exit a room when conflict arises:

"It was their fault."

"Justice is on our side."

"You deserve what you get."

"I know what you need."

"I have the answer for your problem."

Whether we are victim, offender, or peacebuilding practitioner, humility can be hard to sustain when conflict is rising.

When humility becomes a guiding virtue, we begin to question success-driven models of responding and of evaluating responses to harm. Measuring restorative justice by the recidivism rates of offenders, or peacebuilding programs by their efficiency in eliminating violence confines the scope of what it means to be peace to very narrow indicators. Such success-driven models often force us to promise more than we can deliver. They inevitably lead us toward favoring safe and controllable models in which we can predict results.

When humble facilitators don't measure success by predetermined outputs, participants find space to chart their own path. The Kenyan Council of Churches, working in the Rift Valley on a peacebuilding project, couldn't make sense of the linear input-output paradigm of the grant-evaluation form they were supposed to fill out. The whole orientation time did not give space for their local ways of knowing. The absolute terms they were asked to reflect on didn't give space for their traditional humble orientation towards ancestors. So they made up their own way of evaluating peacebuilding that respected those local ways.[19] Humility nurtures the capacity to question the inputs, the outputs, the process, and even the helpfulness of such categories.

Seeing through the lens of humility leads to strategic peacebuilding analysis. Humility removes the pressure to be falsely confident, to pretend to know what is going on, or to have a quick fix to a "simple problem." Humility enhances our capacity to see the complexity of life even if we don't fully understand it. If our humility is inspired by a deep respect for relationships, we are both realistic about our own limitations and at the same time mindful that like everyone else, we are already interconnected with these relationships and therefore have a capacity to contribute to change.

Peacebuilding action that is inspired by humility admits mistakes, starts again, and persistently tries to find another way. Even those who play competitive sports do not assume that their every attempt will be successful. Imagine a soccer player who gives up because her first attempt at scoring does not succeed. Rather she learns from her mistake, and she tries a multitude of strategies, plays, and fakes to open up a new path to the goal. The humility of not expecting success all at once can sustain us and even provoke us to creativity.

Humble action always respects the sacredness of others' lenses and the limitations of our own. When rooted in the

19. Second Action-Reflection Seminar, *Responsive Evaluation of Peacebuilding*.

sacredness of the other, humility does not assume to know what others need or to impose its vision of the world on others. Humility creates the space to learn together and to design together what Gandhi called "experiments with truth."

Ethically Guiding Questions Rooted in *Humility*:

Eliciting Vision Questions: How does humility function within your tradition? How does humility shine a different light on wisdom? What kinds of actions are born out of humility?

Design/Analysis Questions: Do design and analysis nurture a kind of tinkering rather than a solving atmosphere? Is there room to question even one's own insights, and room for the initiatives to move in surprising, even threatening directions?

Intervention Questions: Does the intervention promise more than it can deliver? How do you set a tone of humility? How could intervention be redesigned to reflect what you are learning now?

Evaluation Questions: What were the unintended effects of the intervention? What did you learn about how change happens?

Holding Together Transformation and Humility

Transformation says I can change the world. Humility says I'm not even sure of what I know. The two are not exclusive but must be held together. Humility without some vision of change degenerates into a paralysis of self-pity or radical individualism. Transformation without humility can degenerate into empire building. The two need each other. When transformation and humility are linked, change is sought through listening, empowerment, and holistic vision.

SUMMARY

This chapter has focused on how change happens. I've called it a relational approach to change. In the first part of the chapter, we dealt with questions of *who*: Who is involved in this harm? How can we create caring responses with those involved? The virtue of the generations lens extends our time horizon, enabling us to see patterns through history, focusing on issues of identity, structures, and our ability to survive together on the earth. The second part of the chapter moved on to how we might spark change. The virtues of transformation and humility present us with the dilemma of holding out the hope for radical transformation while at the same time recognizing complexity and our own limitation. Put more simply, this chapter asked: How do we love? How might love inform our practices of peace and justice? The language of love is of course overused. We are not speaking of fleeting emotions here. The kind of love we are speaking of is one that enters into the complexity of the material world and seeks to love the world, to heal the world. What sets this kind of love apart from some others is that this love extends to all creation. Moreover this love cannot be pursued through unloving means. For Christians, because this love is defined by the life of Jesus, this love cannot be seen as a be-nice love or a sweep-it-under-the-carpet love. The love of Jesus disrupted both political, imperial sensibilities and religious, pietistic sensibilities. The virtue pair of care-response and generations lens, and also the pair of transformation and humility, can guide us to engage such a love in our peace and justice practices.

FOUR

The Creative Search for Truth

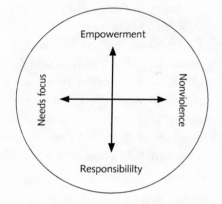

To some extent, any dealing with conflict is a search for truth. Through examining violent criminal behavior, James Gilligan argues that the primary motive of violence is to remove shame and achieve justice.[1] So even violence and injustice are sometimes attempts at seeking truth. It is no wonder that truth is getting a bad name in our society. The pursuit of truth has repeatedly led to violence throughout the ages. Yet the sages keep calling us to seek truth. How do we search for truth without killing truth? Without harming others? Without being

1. Gilligan, *Violence.*

co-opted by untruth? How do we seek truth when everyone has a piece but no one has the whole truth? How do we resist using truth like a sword? This chapter explores some of the virtues that have oriented innovative peacebuilders on this search for truth. Answers and formulas are not offered here. Perhaps answers and formulas are part of the problem as they share some of the same logic as violence. ("I know what you need and I'm going to give it to you whether you want it or not.") Rather this chapter continues to nurture our creative capacity to respectfully enter into conflict and to partner with conflict participants in opening up new (and sometimes old) horizons where we can seek truth, justice, and peace.

The first virtue coupling, needs orientation and non-violence, holds in tension two key elements in what Gandhi would call "experiments with truth." The second virtue coupling, empowerment and responsibility, takes us into territory more likely for social ethics, but these virtues are placed here to be interpreted in light of those that precede them.

NEEDS ORIENTATION AND NONVIOLENCE

Needs Orientation—Justpeace as Meeting Needs

> When institutionalized restorative justice is taken back to indigenous people and their communities, it stops serving their needs and interests. Rather, it becomes a mechanism of coercion and cooptation.[2]
>
> —*Ovide Mercredi, former Grand Chief of the Assembly of First Nations*

2. Mercredi, "Closing Remarks."

There is a grave misconception among some people in the conflict-resolution field that conflict is essentially about miscommunication or poor communication. They say that if we could move beyond our fixed positions and listen to the underlying interests of our opponents, and if we could just learn to listen well and speak well, then we would resolve conflicts. Techniques abound in the conflict-resolution field for listening, speaking, and problem solving through negotiating interests. Yet when a focus on miscommunication is the only lens we use, we blind ourselves to many aspects of conflict, violence, peace, and justice.

As individuals and as groups of human beings, we have many real needs—needs that are nonnegotiable. These include material needs of food, shelter, and water, but also much more. We have basic social, cultural, and spiritual needs. When these needs are blocked through direct violence or through structures that prevent access to or exploration of these needs, then we breed injustice. We need space to explore who we are (social needs), how we relate and create meaning (cultural needs), and how we are connected to the visible and invisible worlds (spiritual needs).[3]

One of the key distinguishing marks of biblical justice is the special attention given to those whose needs are blocked: the resident alien (Deut 24:17), the stranger (Deut 10:17), the oppressed (Eccl 5:8), the widow or orphan (Exod 22:21–22), the poor. Biblical texts also give strong warnings to those in positions to be oppressors: landowners, employers, government leaders, the rich, and those who hoard. Meeting the needs of each member of society is an essential part of justice.

3. Schirch, *Strategic Peacebuilding*.

From the standpoint of interconnectedness, these basic needs are indivisible. Who we are is connected to our relationship with land (material needs), God (spiritual needs), governance (social needs), and the making of meaning (cultural needs). Yet too often we try to divide these needs, ignore them, or substitute foreign needs. Dividing human needs leads to neocolonialist attitudes. Too often the message to Aboriginal peoples is that they should be culturally and spiritually Aboriginal, but that their style of governance (social needs) and their access to resources (material needs) would remain in Western control.[4] In Canada the government has apologized for its policy of racial assimilation that led to forcing children out of their homes and communities and taking them to residential schools. Here physical and sexual abuses were the norm for many students. Moreover they were not allowed to speak their language or practice traditional ways. In taking responsibility for the abuse that happened at these schools, the government initially attempted to compensate for physical and sexual abuse but not initially for cultural abuse. Dividing between basic human needs leads to further oppression.

If we want to find a healing path and to grow in our capacity to build justpeace, we must allow ecological and human needs to be at the center of our peacebuilding efforts. However, too often this is not the case. Rather than holding central the self-articulated needs of those most affected by conflict, we substitute the needs of the powerful. International peace accords often meet the interests (and ego needs) of the leaders and do little for the basic needs of those at the grass

---

4. Alfred, *Peace, Power, Righteousness.*

roots. Criminal legislation of "developed countries" substitutes the state for the victim as the primary object of harm. In both cases, the needs of grassroots people get sidelined as the needs of institutions, leaders, and founders take precedence.

Wise peacebuilding corrects this injustice. Those most affected by harm are invited to play a central role in the transformation of their own conflicts. This means victims, offenders, and communities need spaces to articulate their own needs and to enter into meaningful interaction regarding the other's needs.

A number of key principles follow from needs-oriented peacebuilding. First, flexibility and creativity are vital if our responses to conflict are going to be rooted in the needs of people and communities. Responses to harm that are limited by precedent or preset processes lack the flexibility to be meaningful. A traditional healer in Fiji said it this way: "The healing path only unfolds as you travel it."[5] The path of justpeace must remain ad hoc. If we have too many preconceived ideas of the process and the solution, we will not give enough space to those who have experienced the harm most severely. When our processes and solutions are not rooted in the particular needs of the people involved, they become further tools of alienation.

Second, needs orientation means seeking security through establishing the security, not the insecurity, of the other. When our foreign-policy decisions or our personal choices are based solely on securing our own needs at the expense of the other, we create a violent and unjust world. In contrast, the ethic that is developed through this virtue is one

5. Katz, *Straight Path of the Spirit*, 311.

of friendship. When basic needs are blocked, the potential for violence builds up. When we act in ways that make the other more insecure, we follow a path to greater insecurity for us all. It is not clear what Osama bin Laden's intentions were in smashing the Twin Towers, but it is clear that we have responded in ways that create a breeding ground for terrorists. How many terrorists were created when half a million children were dying in Iraq from the sanctions that followed the Gulf War of 1991? How many terrorists were created when we bombed innocent villages in Afghanistan in 2001? How many terrorists are being created from the occupation of Iraq begun in 2003? Insecurity does not lead to security. It is when we learn to participate in satisfying the basic needs of all parties that a self-sustaining justpeace can be tasted by all. In designing conflict interventions, we must find ways to build internal security through meeting the real needs of the other party.

Third, needs orientation is a category of conflict analysis. Justpeace building must have the capacity to engage greed—both personal and systemic forms. As N. Radhakrishnan notes, "Gandhi experimented with the developments of small autonomous communities, respecting everyone's needs but not for everybody's greed."[6] Our analysis of conflict situations must have the capacity to examine whose basic needs are being excluded and who is responsible for this exclusion. We need to find ways to transform the greed of individuals, the greed of institutions, and the greed of systems. Sharing is a virtue in nearly every wisdom tradition. Justpeace responses transform greed and neglect through sharing.

6. Radhakrishnan, "Gandhi in the Globalised Context."

The Sarvadoya Movement in Sri Lanka is one such example. Even their name means the awakening of all through sharing. Sarvadoya is a Buddhist nongovernmental "development" organization that works on an empowerment village model but demands that development workers tackle what Sarvadoya understands to be the roots of violence, namely, greed and ignorance.[7]

In the United States in cases of capital punishment, needs orientation led to the public's demand that the victim's needs guide the process of sentencing those accused of murder. The new and evolving role of Defense-Initiated Victim Outreach resulted.[8] In this process, building relationships and creating a strategic bridge between victim and offender resulted in the victim's own stated needs becoming the basis for the offender to take responsibility. This is done by incorporating the victim's stated needs into a plea agreement, which in effect sentences the offender to take responsibility for the specific stated needs of the victim. As capital punishment cannot be part of a plea agreement, the offender's life is spared (although there is still mandatory sentencing for murder pleas of guilty). The victim is spared being revictimized through the adversarial process and through constant media coverage. And it is the basic needs of the victim that are at the heart of the sentence.

Attending to the basic needs of those affected by harm is a path to creating powerful peacebuilding and justice-building experiments.

7. http://www.sarvodaya.org/.
8. Krause, "Reaching out to the Other Side."

> **Ethically Guiding Questions Rooted in *Needs Orientation*:**
>
> *Eliciting Vision Questions:* In your tradition, what happens to those who neglect the needs of the vulnerable? Who are the people who call for meeting the needs of all? How does meeting needs relate to justice and security?
>
> *Design/Analysis Questions:* How are those involved in the harm articulating their own basic needs? Whose basic needs are being excluded? Who is responsible for this exclusion?
>
> *Intervention Question:* How can strategies be developed that aim at meeting the basic needs of all involved in the harm?
>
> *Evaluation Questions:* For which groups are basic human needs still being overlooked? Did the intervention further distance anyone from having their basic needs met?

Nonviolence—Exposing Injustice and Discovering Justice

> Truth (satya) implies love, and firmness (agraha) engenders and therefore serves as a synonym for force. I thus began to call the Indian movement satyagraha; that is to say, the force which is born of truth and love or nonviolence.[9]
>
> —*Mahatma Gandhi*

Nonviolence flows out of all the preceding virtues. If interconnectedness is the means and end, then violence can never be a path to justice, because it breaks relationship. When particularity is a virtue, we cannot pursue methods of extinguishing the other. If we seek a response born out of care, we cannot justify violence that fuels hate. If we seek a wise decision that will produce fruit for generations to come, we cannot accept the fragile short-term gains that violence offers. If we take seriously the limits of our knowledge (humility), we cannot make

9. Gandhi, *Satyagraha in South Africa*, 177.

the kind of absolute condemnation that violence assumes. If we are deeply committed to transformation, we must not, through killing, permanently end all hopes of change. If we commit to securing the basic needs of the enemies, we cannot also commit acts of violence against them.

The core of nonviolence is love. Love reflects the end we desire. Love is the only means to that end. Wise peacebuilding is about finding a path of love: to love of self, love of God, love of creation, love of neighbor, love of stranger, even love of enemy. Love is the height and depth of all wisdom. It is the greatest of all commandments.

Yet we discarded love long ago. To those who wanted to rule over others, the political implications of love were too great. So love was spiritualized and romanticized, privatized and trivialized, stripped of its essential core. It was deemed by many to be irrelevant.

So if we can't draw on the creative, transforming power of love, where do we turn? For many people, violence is the instrument of last resort. Others don't wait for the last resort but turn to violence as a preemptive measure. Violence, they believe, will help bring about justice and peace. We have tried this strategy for thousands of years, and our world is getting more and more violent. It is time for a new strategy.

Violence does not fit the justpeace paradigm—whether violence that subjugates, violence that takes revenge, violence that sparks and spurs revolution, or structural violence that systematically denies the basic human needs of others.[10] However, passivity and blind submission also do not fit the justpeace paradigm. Nonviolence is a practical and strategic way both to transform conflict and to wage conflict. It is a way both to reduce violence and to increase justice.

10. Assefa, *Peace and Reconciliation*.

I believe that nonviolence is the most powerful and most common force in human history. I believe that the logic of violence is deeply rooted in our imaginations, in our social and political structures, and in our economic structures. And yet, despite this, our normal way of relating is through nonviolence. Even a soldier spends most of his day acting nonviolently. Usually when we relate to our friends, our families, and our communities we use nonviolent methods of interaction. This type of care and friendship does not need theory to justify it. It is only when we begin to act less than human that we need to go through mental gymnastics and conditioning in order to bypass that very basic and sacred commandment: love.

Generally we accept the language of "just war" but would be shocked by the language of "just rape," "just slavery," or "just murder." However, it seems that justifying violence leads to dehumanization. Dehumanization does not lead to recovering our humanity. Dehumanizing and killing is always a path of alienating and distorting. It is, therefore, a path of untruth. On the other hand, nonviolence is, as Gandhi noted, a force born out of truth and love.[11]

For many reasons, nonviolence is a wise virtue. Let me highlight just a few. Nonviolence

1. is the path of wise peacebuilders. From Jesus to Buddha, nonviolence has an ancient transformative tradition of being the path of truth;

2. shows respect for all life;

3. is consistent with normal virtues of life;

4. lays a firm foundation. Our futures, our dreams, our destinies are intertwined; in the long run, harming others harms us;

11. Gandhi, *Non-Violent Resistence*, 3–36.

5. calls out love rather than hate of the other;

6. reflects the character of beautiful justice;

7. is a quest for truth rather than victory (allows room for the other to be right);

8. is a better long-term strategy, builds rather than undermines relationships;

9. works—we've tried violence for centuries, and it doesn't work;

10. is a powerful method, boasting a strong historical record;

11. empowers grassroots rather than suppressing them;

12. makes logical sense (killing people to show that killing people is wrong doesn't make sense);

13. has great capacity to convert or transform the other, an ability to make friends and soften enemies;

14. has the capacity to break the cycle of violence, stopping rather than fueling recruitment of enemies;

15. is faithful to the way and life of Jesus and to his call to love enemies.

Gene Sharp and the Albert Einstein Institution have done a tremendous job of telling the many stories of massive nonviolent action while at the same time working to understand the dynamics and practical methods of "waging" nonviolence. The historical record is strong, and the strategic options are plentiful.[12] Violence is never a last resort.

Nonviolence calls us to find nonviolent mechanisms for both expressing and handling conflict. It favors cooperative methods such as circles or conferencing over adversarial ones

12. Sharp, *Waging Nonviolent Struggle*.

such as the courts. Doing harm to offenders is not nonviolence. Neither is the offense. Neither is the environment that
created the conditions within which the offense took place.
Needs-oriented nonviolence is concerned with all of these
levels. How do we stop a violent event without perpetuating
the cycles of violence? From the long-term perspective, violence never stops violence. Only nonviolence has the capacity
to disrupt cycles of ongoing violence (crisis) while at the same
time dismantling the (long-term, systemic) institutions of
harm. And we do need intervention on both levels. We need
nonviolent crisis intervention for critical-incident responses,
and we need to nurture whole cultures of peaceful coexistence, economics of nonviolence, and organizations of care.

Ethically Guiding Questions Rooted in *Nonviolence*:

Eliciting Vision Questions: Who in your tradition embodies such nonviolence? What do their lives teach about how we engage nonviolence?
Why is nonviolence practiced in your tradition? Are there limits on how
nonviolence should be practiced?

Design/Analysis Questions: Where are the traditional methods of
nonviolent conflict intervention and how can they be strengthened?
Is there some way of inventing a nonviolent option so that the choice
between violence and nonviolence is a true choice? In what ways are
you participating and giving consent to violent structures? How can
that consent be removed?

Intervention Question: Does this intervention move parties toward
nonviolent ways of expressing and dealing with crisis and with root
causes of violence?

Evaluation Questions: Has the initiative led to the creation of beloved
community, including even enemies? Who has been excluded and feels
bitterness and discontent as a result of this initiative? Is there a way of
meeting their needs?

Holding Together Needs Orientation and Nonviolence

In the past, meeting basic human needs has been linked to violence, both by individuals and the state. A justpeace ethic calls for a different way for both individuals and the state. Rooted in interconnectedness, a caring respect for people, humility, and a desire for deep transformation, justpeace is interested in both basic needs and nonviolence. Meeting basic human and ecological needs without a commitment to nonviolence opens the door to reorganized oppression, to revolutionaries becoming the next dictators.

EMPOWERMENT AND RESPONSIBILITY

Empowerment—Creating Space for Participation

> Victims also need to be empowered. Justice cannot simply be done to and for them. They must feel needed and listened to in the process. Since one dimension of wrong was that they were robbed of power, one dimension of justice is to return power to them.[13]

> —*Howard Zehr*

In the North, there's a traditional Aboriginal teaching about the seven sacred laws. One of these laws, represented by the beaver, is wisdom. One elder spoke of the connection between wisdom and gifts. We all have gifts that must be practiced. These gifts must be brought to the collective because we all need each other. He noted that if the beaver did not use his gifts (his incredible teeth), he would become useless

13. Zehr, *Changing Lenses*, 194.

and die. It is the same for us. If we don't figure out how to find a dynamic place in the larger collective where we can express our voice and offer both our insights and our pain, we will become useless and die. This teaching about wisdom is a teaching about empowerment that arises out of a respect for our interconnectedness and our particularity.

Empowerment is first of all about space to allow meaningful participation in the transformation of your own conflicts.[14] Some say this is the most important goal of peacebuilding.[15] Part of the field of trauma healing is noticing that trauma is not so much created by crisis or conflict as by an inability to complete natural healing cycles.[16] When we are stopped from participating in the processing of our own conflicts, we are traumatized. Sometimes we are stopped by a state system that steals conflicts from communities and individuals in the name of serving the community. Sometimes we are stopped by caring professionals, such as social workers, counselors, and clergy, who interrupt our ability to process our own conflict because they force us to fit their models or theories. Sometimes we are stopped by conflict-resolution professionals who bring us processes, and their well-meaning facilitation robs us of an opportunity to discover our own insights. Sometimes it is our desire to help others that ends up disempowering them. When an egg is about to hatch, if you "help" the chick by opening the egg, the chick will die. It needs to participate in the struggle of birth in order to stay alive. I am not arguing here for an ultimate individual or for an iso-

14. Lederach, *Building Peace*; Zehr, *Changing Lenses*.
15. Kraybill et al., *Peace Skills*.
16. Levine, *Waking the Tiger*.

lationist approach to conflict: quite the opposite. Some have argued that empowerment alone is the key virtue in the social ethics of third-party intervention.[17] However, the kind of empowerment that I am advocating here is the kind that arises out of our particular identity and our interconnectedness. It is an empowerment to meet the needs of all. By receiving space for deep participation in our own conflicts and healing, we become strong again. By rebuilding a sense of meaning, we find our balanced place within the larger whole.

This kind of empowerment comes out of a particular orientation toward power. It is a view that power is essentially relational, based on the consent of people, a consent that can be withdrawn.[18] If the essential character of life is that we are relationally connected while at the same time distinct, it follows that each part of the system needs to participate in its transformation. This means that top-down, coercive, imposed power is rarely healthy or healing. One is not brought to justpeace by some coercive means. Rather justpeace is discovered together.

Practitioners use this view of power and empowerment both as a vision and as a strategic means. Mass nonviolent action is essentially the withdrawal of the consent of the masses from an oppressive system. National economies only function when people go to work and make purchases. Strikes and boycotts are strategies of withdrawing consent through withdrawing participation. Wise restorative-justice practice involves creating space for those most affected by harm (the victim, the offender, the family, the community or communi-

17. Bermant, *Ethics of Social Intervention.*
18. Sharp, *Waging Nonviolent Struggle.*

ties) so that they can participate meaningfully in all stages of
the transformation of the harm. This is a form of cooperative
power sharing. It requires that both the state and the many
helping professions recognize that conflicts belong to those
most affected by the harm. It requires creating space for those
who are in the setting and are already working toward justpeace, rather than imposing external measures.

So what are participants empowered to do? First, participants are empowered to choose how and if they want to
participate. In the Christian gospels, Jesus often asks a cu-
rious question of those who seek him: "Do you want to be
healed?" This or a similar question gives space to the seeker
to explore longings and desires. There is wisdom in this approach. Coercing people to heal rarely works. At some level,
people need to choose that they want to work constructively
at the conflict before them. Sometimes this choosing comes
from voluntary participation at the beginning of the process,
as in most restorative-justice approaches. However, sometimes a person makes the decision that she wants to hear
truth only after the community has been trying for years to
break through her lies and denial, as has sometimes been the
case in Hollow Water.[19]

Having received space to begin participating in their
own healing, participants are next empowered to help create the process for dealing with the harms done to them. The
process must reflect our particularity, our distinct identity,
and the basic needs at issue. It is not enough to invite participation in a preexisting process even if the process seems

19. See Ross, *Return to the Teachings*, 29–39; see also Sawatsky, *Ethic
of Traditional Communities*.

cooperative, e.g., as in mediation. It is often helpful to give those in conflict some options for processes, but if we are interested in nurturing paths of justpeace that have the capacity to transform institutions and imaginations, we must not limit ourselves to preset processes of how to deal with the conflict. Processes are always carriers of cultural-political assumptions. One example of this is the South African Zwelethemba Peacemaker Model. In this model, local peace committees are created of between five and twenty local people (often in very poor settings) who agree to a "code of good practice," which informs the imagination of what happens in these committees. These informal, nonstate committees respond to harms in their community—both episodic and structural harms. But they do not have a preset process or even a declared facilitator. They work together with the community to determine what should be done and how it should be done.[20]

Third, participants are empowered to give voice to their experience. To share one's story and to have it taken seriously is a very important part of healing and empowerment. When we tell our story, we name what happens to us in ways that make sense to us, as opposed to fitting a preconceived typology of harm or crime. We name what is happening, we communicate the impacts of harm, and, somehow, in the process, we create meaning. Victims need this space for exploration. Offenders need this space. Communities need this space. These explorations are all interconnected. Often hearing the impacts told firsthand from the mouth of a victim

20. Froestad and Shearing, "Conflict Resolution in South Africa"; Cartwright and Jenneker, "Governing Security."

has the power to transform the estrangement of the offender. Sometimes hearing firsthand the story of the offender breaks a logjam for a victim who is paralyzed in fear of the other. So we are empowered both to give voice to our story and to hear the other person.

Fourth, participants are empowered to contribute to the outcome. For an outcome to be a healing path, participants need to take some ownership of it. It should not surprise us that the rulings of judges imposed on offenders, victims, and communities are rarely healing. Meaningful empowerment includes victims' and their communities' coming together to create a plan for restoration and healing. Empowerment increases when the community is accountable for monitoring implementation.

Fifth, empowerment includes creating space for participants to return to rightfully balanced relationship in community. Left on our own, isolated, we are not empowered; we are depressed and lonely, liable to shrivel up and die. This is true for victims, for offenders and for whole communities. We are created for connection. Empowerment brings us back into beautiful connection.

Empowerment in this context comes as something of a wild beast. It involves sharing power without guarantees on the process or outcome. Too often our preset processes advantage the powerful and undermine the less powerful. Empowerment as a key virtue means remaining sensitive and flexible in light of these potential power imbalances. Empowerment is yet another reminder that justpeace is not static but dynamic and sometimes disruptive.

Ethically Guiding Questions Rooted in *Nonviolence*:

Eliciting Vision Questions: Who empowers people in your tradition? What are people empowered for? What happens when empowerment is absent? How is empowerment connected to the virtues that come before?

Design/Analysis Questions: Whose voice is being excluded? Are the people most intimately involved in the conflict also involved in the design and analysis of its transformation?

Intervention Question: Does the intervention strategy contribute to the ability of the relatively powerless people to participate and define the way toward justpeace?[21]

Evaluation Questions: Are those on the margins participating in, advocating, or supporting the type of interventions being evaluated? What do victims think? What do offenders think? What do their communities of origin think?

Responsibility—Accountability for the Ripples

> The salvation of this human world lies nowhere else than in the human heart, in the human power to reflect, in human meekness, and in human responsibility.[22]
>
> —*Vaclav Havel*

Interconnectedness creates responsibility. We don't live in isolation. The world is relationship: all is connected. For good

21. Modification of an intervention question from Laue and Cormick in Bermant, et al., *Ethics of Social Intervention*. Laure and Cormick saw empowerment as the essential principle for ethical intervention in social conflict. Justpeace ethics highlights empowerment within a larger context.

22. Havel, "Speech."

or for bad our actions ripple across the interconnected web of relationships. If we live, produce, and purchase as if the earth doesn't matter, it will eventually die. Similarly, if we live as if our neighbors don't matter, they will suffer greatly. And not just they—for if our neighbors suffer, we suffer. Whether or not we see it and acknowledge it, "injustice anywhere is injustice everywhere." This deep interconnection, then, creates responsibility. We cannot simply judge our actions by what they appear to do for us. Actions are judged by the effect they have on the rest of the web of relationships, by what they do for others.

When we act in ways that harm relationships, we create a special responsibility to make things right to others. Healing is about addressing harm and cultivating life.

Taking responsibility is different from guilt. Guilt is an inward self-orientation that paralyzes the soul. It says, "I was wrong. I broke this rule. I screwed up." Unprocessed guilt leads to shame. Shame says, "I am a failure. I am useless. I am dead inside." Both guilt (the failure of doing) and shame (the failure of being) reflect essentially on the self.[23] Ironically, it is often this same self-centered attitude that leads to the harm in the first place. When we harm others, we take what looks like a short-term gain for ourselves at the expense of the others. No wonder that guilt and shame paralyze. They reflect the same logic that caused the harm. By contrast, responsibility orients the heart toward the other. Where guilt leads to punishment and shame, responsibility leads to making things right for the other person. Whereas we degenerate inwardly because of guilt, we unfold outwardly through responsibility. Taking

23. Potter-Efron and Potter-Efron, *Letting Go of Shame*.

responsibility releases guilt while at the same time creating a new horizon for healing in both the doer and the receiver. Through responsibility, acts of shame can be transformed into courageous acts of love. Actions motivated by our need to relieve guilt rarely have this potential. Because they are still self-centered actions, they are still very dangerous.

Taking responsibility does not just mean addressing a past incident of harm. It also involves addressing the patterns of the past and the patterns of the future. Incidents have roots in patterns and momentums of relationships. Sometimes these are not the sole responsibility of the one who inflicted harm in a specific incident. But we must nurture the capacity to address both the micro- and macropatterns that lead to harmful decisions. Otherwise we are just applying bandages without dealing with the depth or the source of the harming. Taking responsibility means looking both to root causes and toward shared futures. To rebuild trust in relationships and in the future, those who have been harmed need to know this will not happen again. When we punish offenders and lock them away, we nurture a culture of fear, because victims and communities are not given the opportunity to recognize root causes and future intentions. When we don't know why harm happened or what will happen in the future, we slowly become paralyzed by fear and despair:

"When will it happen again? This is a violent place. There's nothing we can do." When we become dominated by this fear and despair, we lose our own ability to be compassionate or to take responsibility. This creates a cycle of violence.

Responsibility, then, is not just a personal virtue. Responsibility also has corporate, systemic, and communal dimensions. Those of us in the West live in cultures that discourage taking responsibility. We have long habits of shutting away in institutions those whom we have a responsibility to care for: hospitals for the sick and dying, seniors' homes for the elderly, welfare programs for the poor, prisons for those who harm, asylums for the mentally broken. When we build separate buildings and hire specific professionals to deal with those who are most afflicted in our society, we fail to nurture compassion or responsibility at the grassroots level. Rather than caring for the stranger, we develop deep habits of looking the other way. This is very dangerous. We lose our own ability to love, to learn, and to return to a healing path. Policies like being "tough on crime" are really policies of nonresponsibility because they are fed by fear, and they breed fear in both communities and offenders. And fear does not lead us back to responsibility. Being more cruel and alienating to offenders is a stumbling block to healing for victims, for communities, and for offenders alike. Such policies of nonresponsibility make us all suffer very deeply.

So how do we nurture cultures where people take responsibility for their actions? This is a key question for peacebuilders. We must learn how to encourage our culture to take responsibility for the mess we help to create. This ethic applies to big businesses in their environmental and socioeconomic impacts as much as it does to criminals in the human and material impacts of their harm. As long as we believe that justice is about balancing harm for harm, of dealing out punishment for guilt, we will encourage the nonresponsibility of offenders as they try to evade punishment. After all, who would want to face that kind of ugly justice? As long as we believe that truth is unveiled through an adversarial fight between opponents who reflect the same dynamic of untruth, we will not nurture the type of compassion that leads to responsibility. It is only when we learn something of the beauty of justice that we will find a way to nurture cultures of responsibility. Taking responsibility for past harms gives something wonderful back to both offenders and victims. This "something" has to do with integrity, truthfulness, and compassion. It has to do with finding ourselves again, that center that allows us to lift our heads, to look deeply into the other person, and to not be ashamed.

Responsibility is a path to justpeace. We cannot wait for justpeace to arrive before we begin to take responsibility. We will never get there that way. The compassionate future of justpeace arrives as we learn to walk this path even when it seems that others are not.

Ethically Guiding Questions Rooted in *Responsibility*:

Eliciting Vision Questions: Who is responsible for harm? How do people take responsibility? Who is responsible for peace? For justice? How is responsibility practiced as we move through each day?

Design/Analysis Questions: "Who has been hurt? What are their needs? Whose obligations are these?"[24] How do you create space for compassionate encounters?

Intervention Question: Are participants encouraged to take responsibility for past and current hurts? Are victims, offenders, and communities given the opportunity to grow strong through taking responsibility?

Evaluation Questions: Can you see fruit from taking responsibility? What dynamics are stopping people from listening deeply to the other and taking responsibility? How can these dynamics be creatively addressed?

---

24. Zehr, *Little Book of Restorative Justice*, 21.

Holding Together Empowerment and Responsibility

Empowerment without responsibility sees freedom as doing whatever one wants. Responsibility without empowerment is like living with a dictator. Empowerment with responsibility invites you to participate in the transformative justpeace dance. Linking these virtues says that both your needs and your care for the other are important.

SUMMARY

In this chapter we have explored how good justice work and peacebuilding spark creative searches for truth. This creative search for truth is guided by these two virtue pairs: needs orientation and nonviolence on the one hand, and empowerment and responsibility on the other. When we find ways of securing the needs of others (including the needs of the earth) through nonviolent means, we discover that we are the path of justpeace and truth. When we find ways to develop practices of giving empowerment and taking responsibility, we find that we are like the happy beaver of traditional Aboriginal teaching—knowing our place, using our special gift, and enjoying life. But when the empowerment-responsibility pair is absent, we stop using our gifts, we forget our place, we believe that we do not matter, and the path of truth seems like some dark lie. Putting these virtues into practice requires great creativity and courage. Justpeace informed by these virtues is a search for truth, belonging, and fulfillment.

FIVE

Cocreating a Beautiful Deep Justice

> In my view, developing inner peace, on which
> lasting—and therefore—meaningful happiness is
> dependent, is like any other task in life: we have
> to identify its causes and conditions and then
> diligently set about cultivating them. This we find
> entails a two-pronged approach. On the one hand,
> we need to guard against factors which obstruct it.
> On the other, we need to cultivate those which are
> conducive to it.[1]
>
> —*Dalai Lama*

> If then the light in you is darkness, how great is the
> darkness!
>
> —*Jesus* (Matt 6:23)

Justice is not ugly. It is not a sword or a burden or something
we would do well to flee from. This book tries to recover a
beautiful vision of justice rooted in the very character of life,
and to offer hints of wisdom for peacebuilders on the journey
of becoming justpeace, of becoming the end we desire.

1. Dalai Lama, *Ethics for the New Millennium*, 57–58.

85

Gandhi says we must be the change we want to see. Thich Nhat Hanh says that there is no way to peace; peace is the way, that is, we need to be peace in every step. Jesus, whom some call the Prince of Peace, says "I am the . . . life" (John 14:6). Each one points to our present being, the fabric of our existence, the present moment, as the canvas on which peace can live. It is in the fabric of our being that we need to "taste and see" such a justpeace (Psalm 34:8).

Out of listening to practitioners of justice and peace and to teachers of wisdom, I have tried to highlight key virtues or characteristics of justpeace and to offer some suggestions on how, as the Dalai Lama says, to "guard against factors which obstruct" justpeace and also to "cultivate [factors] which are conducive" to it.[2] The following chart summarizes some of these themes.

	Restorative Virtues	Nonrestorative Virtues
Interconnectedness	Interdependence Holistic View Networking Power Cooperative Partnership	Autonomy Dualistic View Hierarchal Power Adversarial Competition
Particularity	Diversity Contextuality Elicitive Approach	Assimilation Universality Prescriptive Approach
Personal Care-Response	Respect Caring Response	Objectification Rules/Rights Response

2. Ibid., 58.

	Restorative Virtues	**Nonrestorative Virtues**
Generational Lens	Discernment of Root Causes Communal Responsibility Accountability Storying and Restorying	Discernment of Symptoms Individual Responsibility Punishment Focusing on Facts
Transformation	Patience Morality Permitted conflict Change of System	Immediacy Amorality Suppressed conflict Defense of System
Humility	Vulnerability Humility Self-Doubt Servantly Facilitation	Strength Omniscience Confidence Expert Leadership
Needs Orientation	Participation Focus on Needs Listening Stance	Subjection Focus on Power or Status Telling/Assuming Stance
Nonviolence	Love of the Enemy Life-giving Organizing	Hatred of the Enemy Structural Violence
Empowerment	Voice Inclusion Flexible Process	Silence Exclusion Rigid Process
Responsibility	Acknowledgment Restitution Responsibility	Denial Punishment Guilt

The chart above may overstate the case by polarizing virtues that are not actually opposites. For example the value of inclusion, the capacity to be open, is only meaningful if it is connected more positively to exclusion, a capacity to be closed. However, we need to find ways of naming those aspects of our life that obstruct justpeace while at the same time cultivating those aspects that nurture it. Sometimes we get these virtues mixed up, or we accept vices as if they are virtues. Our willingness to accept violence, pain, and shame as tools of peace and justice is one such example. The words from Jesus at the start of this chapter remind us of our tendency to accept darkness for light. Correctly naming that which obstructs justpeace and that which nurtures it is a very important part of peacebuilding. This justpeace guide tries to reorient us toward a justice that coexists with peace, healing, structural change, and generational patterns.

This justpeace guide is not a manual of solutions. There is no how-to manual of justpeace solutions. Justpeace doesn't work like that. It is far more dynamic, transformative, and creative than any manual could grasp. Justpeace nurtures both a compassion that compels us to engage with the suffering world and a respect for the other that stops us from "solutioning" the world to death. Justpeace does not offer preset solutions; neither does it offer guarantees of success. What it does offer is a way back to being fully who we are, fully human, fully particular, fully connected.

The guide is not designed so that we can be calculated and formulaic in our approaches to peace and justice. Simply applying all "the rules" will not lead to the desired results. The virtues identified here are found within the character and imagination of grassroots peacebuilders. They are markers of the kind of people we need to become. They are markers of character and imagination. I have tried to show how such an imagination touches the work of restorative justice and peacebuilding by focusing on how this character and imagination might influence the design, intervention, and evaluation of responses to harm. However, the first focus of transformation is our character and imagination, learning to see, feel, taste, and indeed *be* in new (and old) ways. As peacebuilders, we must ask how we can provoke ourselves and our communities to nurture and embody such marks of imagination.

This type of beautiful justice is not found on the distant edges of a compromising choice governed by rules and rights. Rather it is located near the heart of life itself. It calls us to root our lives (including the design, intervention, and evaluation of our peacebuilding activities) in the very character of the justpeace we hope to experience. This is not a new strategy but one that draws on ancient wisdom and the current practice of peacebuilding. The key questions are

- Are we focused on the core qualities of life itself?

- Are we asking the right questions to nurture our capacity to co-create this beautiful justice?

Communities with a distinct identity need to answer these questions for themselves and to continue to interact with distinct communities unlike their own. We don't need common practices of peacebuilding around the world. Life is too diverse to be limited to a few universal practices. But we do need to nurture our capacity to connect compassionately with the other and to transform ourselves to seek truth and harmony in the vast, interconnected world. For this to happen, distinct communities must return to their own stories of faith and life, to their own narrative.[3] A return to their teachings to find resources for such a beautiful justice may well

---

3. Ross, *Return to the Teachings*.

breathe life, diversity and healthy conflict into their dialogue on a justpeace ethic.

Of course traditional faith communities have sometimes been bearers of violence and oppression. My own Christian tradition is one of the worst in this light. But when we return to these traditions and look for wisdom on how we shall live in the present, wisdom abounds. Chris Marshall argues that since God's very character is a loving justice, those who are created in God's image, namely all of humanity, must be agents of justice.[4] From this perspective, even when people persist in responding with injustice, we must always respond to the image of God in the other. Perhaps it is for this reason that the prophet Amos warns people that "without a commitment to justice, all other means of worshipping God . . . are bankrupt" (see Amos 5:21–24).[5]

Some will see such a justpeace ethical guide as too complex. It is complex. But so is the beauty of a sunset, the life of a little child, the suffering of loss. Life is complex. One of the most important practices of peacebuilders is to find ways to make friends with complexity.[6] This justpeace-ethics guide tries to find ways of making friends with complexity without giving in to paralysis. The virtue pair of humility and transformation is very important in this light. Humility ensures we see the complexity, and removes the pressure to create a one-stop solution. Transformation commits us to particular paths of learning and change. The wonderful and sometimes frightening insight of justpeace is that we are invited as cocreators to live out in the flesh, in this world, the fullness of life. It

4. Marshall, *Little Book of Biblical Justice*, 26.

5. Ibid, 30.

6. Lederach, *Little Book of Conflict Transformation*, 53–54.

is within our ability. Our actions and our inactions have real consequences, even if we cannot see them.

The Buddhist peacebuilder Thich Nhat Hanh often states it this way: "The kingdom of God, the Pure Land of the Buddha is available, and we should be able to live in such a way that every day we can get in touch with the wonders of life and be happy."[7] What he is trying to orient us towards is that same thing Jesus tried to orient his disciples toward when he told them to pray: "[May] your kingdom come on earth as it is in heaven" (Matt 6:10). It is possible for us to live taste and see the kingdom of God in the here and now. It is possible to transform our practices of peace and justice in this light. This is why Jesus said, "The kingdom of God has come near" (Mark 1:16).

Some will no doubt see such an ethic as naïve and idealist. Justpeace ethics does not come from my imagination. It is not a theoretical or intellectual exercise based in the ideas of writers. It comes from the ground. It comes from those who are already practicing such a justice, such a peace. For each virtue I pointed toward ways that people are already putting this ethic into practice. This is an ethic that begins with practice and then in hindsight tries to find ways of talking about itself. Justpeace ethics is already lived out in practice in the modern world, in situations of profound violence and suffering. This is a source of great joy and hope. However, deepening our awareness of the beauty of justice also deepens our awareness of where beauty is not practiced and of the conditions that stifle beautiful justice. The journey into beautiful justice is also a journey into suffering. Justpeace is

7. Hanh, "Our Own Refuge."

found and practiced in the midst of suffering and violence. As peacebuilders and justice workers we must relocate ourselves to these places of suffering, not so much to bring justpeace to them, but to discover justpeace within and between each of them.

We hope that by sharing our best insights into what is at the heart of life, and how we might live and be those qualities in the midst of a suffering world, we can spark wise and strategic justpeace transformation. This is a creative, sometimes painful, but deeply joyful task. Let us be justpeace.

Bibliography

Alfred, Taiaiake. *Peace, Power, Righteousness: An Indigenous Manifesto.* Don Mills, ON: Oxford University Press, 1999.

Assefa, Hizkias. *Peace and Reconciliation as a Paradigm: A Philosophy of Peace and Its Implications on Conflict, Governance, and Economic Growth in Africa.* Nairobi: African Peacebuilding and Reconciliation Network, 1993.

Bermant, Gordon, et al. *The Ethics of Social Intervention.* The Series in Clinical and Community Psychology. Washington DC: Hemisphere Publishing Corporation, distributed solely by Halsted Press, 1978.

Boff, Leonardo. *Cry of the Earth, Cry of the Poor.* New York: Orbis, 1997.

Canada. *The Four Circles of Hollow Water.* The Aboriginal Peoples Collection, APC 15 CA (1997). Ottawa: Solicitor General Canada, Aboriginal Corrections Policy Unit, 1997.

Cartwright, John, and Madeleine Jenneker. "Governing Security: A Working Model in South Africa." Peace Committee paper presented at the meeting called A New Decade of Criminal Justice in South Africa, Gordon's Bay, Western Cape, South Africa, February 7–8, 2005.

Cayley, D. (2000). Ivan Illich on the corruption of Christianity. Ideas. D. Cayley. Canada, Canadian Broadcasting Corporation.

Certeau, Michel de. *The Practice of Everyday Life.* Translated by Steven Rendall. Berkeley: University of California Press, 1984.

Christie, Nils. "Conflict as Property." *British Journal of Criminology* 17 (1977) 1–5.

Couture, Joseph. *A Cost-Benefit Analysis of Hollow Water's Community Holistic Circle Healing Process.* Aboriginal Peoples Collection, APC 20 CA (2001). Ottawa: Solicitor General Canada, 2001. Online: http://www.sgc.gc.ca/EPub/AboCor/eAPC2001/eAPC2001.htm.

Dalai Lama XIV. *Ethics for the New Millennium*. New York: Riverhead, 1999.

Freire, Paulo. *Pedagogy of the Oppressed*. New York: Herder and Herder, 1970.

Froestad, Jan, and Clifford Shearing. "Conflict Resolution in South-Africa: A Case Study." In *The Handbook of Restorative Justice*, edited by Gerry Johnstone and Daniel W. Van Ness, 534–56. Cullompton, UK: Willan 2007.

Gandhi, Mahatma. *Satyagraha in South Africa*. Translated by V. G. Desai. Madras: Ganesan, 1938.

———. *Non-violent Resistance (Satyagraha)*. Mineola, N.Y.: Dover, 2001.

Gilligan, James. *Violence: Reflections on a Western Epidemic*. Forensic Focus 18. Philadelphia, PA: Jessica Kingsley, 1999.

Hallman, David. *Ecotheology: Voices from South and North*. New York: Orbis, 2002.

Hanh, Thich Nhat. *For a Future to Be Possible: Buddhist Ethics for Everyday Life*. Berkeley: Parallax, 2007.

———. *Fragrant Palm Leaves, Journals 1962–1966*. Translated by Mobi Warren. Berkeley: Parallax, 1998.

———. "How to Discover Our Own Refuge." Dharma talk given in Plum Village, France, on July 11, 2005. Online: http://www.plumvillage.org/HTML/dharmatalks/html/howtodiscoverourownrefuge.html.

———. *Peace Is Every Step: The Path of Mindfulness in Everyday Life*. New York: Bantam, 1991.

Harris, M. Kay. "Moving into the New Millennium: Toward a Feminist Vision of Justice." In *Criminology as Peacemaking*, edited by Harold Pepinsky and Richard Quinney, 83–97. Indianapolis: Indiana University Press, 1991.

Hauerwas, Stanley. *A Community of Character: Toward a Constructive Christian Social Ethic*. Notre Dame: University of Notre Dame Press, 1981.

Havel, Vaclav. "Speech before the United States Congress." *Washington Post*, February 22, 1990, A28.

Huebner, Chris. *A Precarious Peace: Yoderian Explorations on Theology, Knowledge and Identity*. Scottdale, PA: Herald, 2006.

Illich, Ivan, and David Cayley. *The Corruption of Christianity: Ivan Illich on Gospel, Church and Society*. A transcript of three episodes of the

Canadian Radio Broadcasting Corporation show "Ideas." Toronto: CBC, 2000.

—. *Deschooling Society*. World Perspectives 44. New York: Harper and Row, 1971.

Katz, Richard. *The Straight Path of the Spirit: Ancestral Wisdom and Healing Traditions in Fiji*. Rochester, VT: Park Street, 1999.

King, Martin Luther Jr. "The Birth of a New Nation." Speech delivered at Bethel Baptist Church, Montgomery, Alabama, 1957. Online: http://www.stanford.edu/group/King/speeches/pub/The_birth_of_a_new_nation.html.

—. "Letter from Birmingham Jail." In *Why We Can't Wait*, 64–84. New York: Harper & Row, 1963. Online: http://www.stanford.edu/group/King/popular_requests/frequentdocs/birmingham.pdf.

—. "Nonviolence and Racial Justice." In *A Testament of Hope: The Essential Writings of Martin Luther King Jr.*, edited by James Melvin Washington, 5–9. San Francisco: Harper & Row, 1986.

Krause, Tammy. "Reaching Out to the Other Side: Defense-Based Victim Outreach in Capital Cases." In *Wounds That Do Not Bind*, edited by James R. Acker and David R. Karp, 379–96. Durham, NC: Carolina Academic Press, 2006.

Kraybill, Ron, with Alice Frazer Evans and Robert A. Evans. *Peace Skills: A Manual for Community Mediators*. San Francisco: Jossey-Bass, 2001.

Lederach, John Paul. *Building Peace: Sustainable Reconciliation in Divided Societies*. Washington DC: United States Institute of Peace Press, 1997.

—. "Justpeace: The Challenge of the 21st century." In *People Building Peace*, edited by Paul van Tongeren, 27–36. Utrecht, Netherlands: European Centre for Conflict Prevention, 1999.

—. *The Little Book of Conflict Transformation*. The Little Books of Justice & Peacebuilding. Intercourse, PA: Good Books, 2003.

—. *The Moral Imagination: The Art and Soul of Building Peace*. New York: Oxford University Press, 2005.

—. *Preparing for Peace: Conflict Transformation across Cultures*. Syracuse Studies on Peace and Conflict Resolution. Syracuse: Syracuse University Press, 1995.

————. "Truth and Mercy, Justice and Peace." In Mediation and Facilitation Training Manual, edited by C. Schrock-Shenk, 37–38. Akron, PA: Mennonite Conciliation Services, 2000.

Lee, Gloria. "Defining Traditional Healing." In *Justice as Healing: Indigenous Ways, Writings, on Community Peacemaking and Restorative Justice from the Native American Law Center*, edited by Wanda D. McCaslin, 98–107. St. Paul, MN: Living Justice, 2005.

————. "The Newest Old Gem: Family Group Conferencing." In *Justice as Healing: Indigenous Ways, Writings, on Community Peacemaking and Restorative Justice from the Native American Law Center*, edited by Wanda D. McCaslin, 308–12. St. Paul MN: Living Justice, 2005.

Levine, Peter, with Ann Frederick. *Waking the Tiger: Healing Trauma*. Berkeley: North Atlantic, 1997.

MacIntyre, Alasdair. *After Virtue: A Study in Moral Theory*. 3d edition. Notre Dame: University of Notre Dame Press, 2007.

MacRae, Allan, and Howard Zehr. *The Little Book of Family Group Conference: New Zealand Style*. The Little Books of Justice & Peacebuilding. Intercourse, PA: Good Books, 2004.

Marshall, Christopher D. *The Little Book of Biblical Justice*. The Little Books of Justice & Peacebuilding. Intercourse, PA: Good Books, 2005.

Mercredi, Ovide. "Concluding Remarks." Paper presented at the Conference on Restorative Justice, Winnipeg, Manitoba, September 24–28, 2001.

Moltmann, Jürgen. *Creating a Just Future: The Politics of Peace and the Ethics of Creation in a Threatened World*. London: SCM, 1989.

Newell, J. Philip. *Each Day & Each Night: Celtic Prayers from Iona*. Revised edition. Glasgow: Wild Goose, 2003.

Potter-Efron, Patricia, and Ronald Potter-Efron. *Letting Go of Shame*. Center City, MN: Hazelden, 1989.

Pranis, Kay, et al. *Peacemaking Circles: From Crime to Community*. St. Paul, MN: Living Justice, 2003.

Radhakrishnan, N. "Gandhi in the Globalised Context." In *Gandhian Alternative to Contemporary Problems*, edited by Anil Dutta Mishra et al., 28–44. Delhi: Abhijeet, 2004. Online: http://www.mkgandhi.org/articles/Radhakrishnan.htm.

Ross, Rupert. *Dancing with a Ghost: Exploring Indian Reality*. Toronto: Penguin, 2006.

————. *Returning to the Teachings: Exploring Aboriginal Justice*. Toronto: Penguin, 1996.

Sawatsky, Jarem. *The Ethic of Traditional Communities and the Spirit of Healing Justice: Studies from Hollow Water, Plum Village and the Iona Community*. London: Jessica Kingsley, forthcoming, 2009.

————. "A JustPeace Ethic: Dancing Our Way Back to Humanity." Online: http://www.emu.edu/ctp/ethic.pdf.

————. "Restorative Values: Where Means and Ends Converge." Paper presented at the Sixth International Conference on Restorative Justice, Vancouver, British Columbia, June 1–4 2003. Online: http://www.sfu.ca/cfrj/popular.html.

Schirch, Lisa. *The Little Book of Strategic Peacebuilding*. The Little Books of Justice & Peacebuilding. Intercourse, PA: Good Books, 2004.

Second Action-Reflection Seminar. *Strategic and Responsive Evaluation of Peacebuilding: Towards a Learning Model*. Nairobi: NPI-Africa and the NCCK-CPBD Project, 2001.

Shapiro, Fred. Comment posted on Quoteland.com July 26, 2007. Online: http://forum.quoteland.com/1/OpenTopic?a=tpc&s=586192041&f=099191541&m=1541945383.

Sharp, Gene. *Waging Nonviolent Struggle: 20th Century Practice and 21st Century Potential*. Boston: Porter Sargent, 2005.

Sivell-Ferri, Christine. "The Ojibwa Circle: Tradition and Change." *In Four Circles of Hollow Water*, edited by the Ministry of the Solicitor General of Canada. Aboriginal Peoples Collection. Ottawa: Solicitor General Canada Aboriginal Corrections Policy Unit, 1997. Online: http://ww2.ps-sp.gc.ca/publications/abor_corrections/199703_e.pdf.

Thakur, Shanti, director. *Circles*. Montreal: National Film Board of Canada, 1997.

Umbreit, Mark S., and the Center for Restorative Justice & Peacemaking. *The Handbook of Victim Offender Mediation: An Essential Guide to Practice and Research*. San Francisco: Jossey-Bass, 2001.

United Nations Economic and Social Council. *Basic Principles on the Use of Restorative Justice Programmes in Criminal Matters*. New York: United Nations Economic and Social Council, 2002. Online: http://www.pficjr.org/programs/un/ecosocresolution.

Wheatley, Margaret J., and Myron Kellner-Rogers. *A Simpler Way*. Provo: Berrett-Koehler, 1999.

Witte, John. "Between Sanctity and Depravity: Law and Human Nature in Martin Luther's Two Kingdoms." *Villanova Law Review* 48 (2003) 727–62.

Yoder, John Howard. *The Politics of Jesus : Vicit Agnus Noster.* 2d edition. Grand Rapids: Eerdmans, 1994.

Zehr, Howard. *Changing Lenses, A Christian Peace Shelf Selection.* Scottdale, PA: Herald, 1990.

———. "Justice That Heals: The Practice." *Stimulus* 2 (1994) 69–74.

———. "Justice That Heals: The Vision." *Stimulus* 2 (1994) 5–11.

———. *The Little Book of Restorative Justice.* The Little Books of Justice & Peacebuilding. Intercourse, PA: Good Books, 2002.